D0744728

Landscapes of
LA PALMA
AND EL HIERRO

a countryside guide
Seventh edition

Noel Rochford
updated by Conny Spelbrink

SUNFLOWER BOOKS

Seventh edition © 2015
Sunflower Books™
PO Box 36160
London SW7 3WS, UK
www.sunflowerbooks.co.uk

Sunflower Books and
'Landscapes' are Registered
Trademarks.

ISBN 978-1-85691-462-8

Windmill near Las Tricias (Walk 15)

Important note to the reader

We have tried to ensure that the descriptions and maps in this book are error-free at press date. The book will be updated, where necessary, whenever future printings permit. It will be very helpful for us to receive your comments (sent in care of the publishers, please) for the updating of future printings.

We also rely on those who use this book — especially walkers — to take along a good supply of common sense when they explore. Conditions change fairly rapidly in the Canary Islands, and *storm damage or bulldozing may make a route unsafe at any time*. If the route is not as we outline it here, and your way ahead is not secure, return to the point of departure. *Never attempt to complete a tour or walk under hazardous conditions!* Please read carefully the notes on pages 36 to 41, as well as the introductory comments at the beginning of each tour and walk (regarding road conditions, equipment, grade, distances and time, etc). Explore *safely*, while at the same time respecting the beauty of the countryside.

Cover photograph: enormous colonies of ferns at Los Tilos (Walk 4)
Title page: sabina, a native juniper

Photographs: Noel Rochford, except for pages 2, 18-19, 24, 75
(middle), 77, 84, 94-5, 106, 111, 120-1 and cover (Conny Spelbrink)
Maps: Sunflower Books, based on 1:50,000 Spanish military maps (with
permission of the Servicio Geográfico del Ejército)
Drawings: Sharon Rochford
A CIP catalogue record for this book is available from the British Library.
Printed and bound in England: Short Run Press, Exeter

✿ Contents

3

Market in Santa Cruz

Preface

For most tourists in Britain, the Canary Islands mean Tenerife, Gran Canaria, Lanzarote and Fuerteventura. But there are actually seven islands in the archipelago. Lesser-known La Gomera, La Palma and El Hierro are still utopias for nature lovers. They are as yet virtually unspoilt.

They lack the fine glistening beaches of the more popular islands, and this may be their saving grace. It's unlikely that mainstream tourism will ever reach them. Great news for those of us who seek peace and quiet.

In natural beauty, La Palma rivals all the other islands put together. Its immense, abyss-like crater, the Caldera de Taburiente (which geologists now refer to as an enormous landslide), is one of the largest of its kind in the world. Deep within its pine-speckled, towering walls is a year-round abundance of water — gushing streams, boisterous cascades, and a plummeting waterfall. Outside the crater, high on the cloud-catching hillsides, two million-year-old laurel forests grow as dense as jungle. In the southern half of the island, hills pitted with volcanic craters, and mini-deserts of black *lapilli* speak of the island's volcanic past. This stark, striking landscape, all the more dramatic for its stabs of volcanic reds, oranges, and yellows, is far removed from the lush and verdant, tree-clad north.

Landing on El Hierro by boat many years ago, I wondered what I had let myself in for. Before me stood a dried-up, sprawling mountain of rock, rising straight from the sea, treeless and barren. Tired stone walls stretched half-heartedly across steep sea slopes ... the only hint of civilization. But day by day the island's charms revealed themselves: dramatic cliff top views, highland pastures shrouded in mist, countryside littered with volcanic cones, a maze of stone walls, turquoise-green rock pools, delightful rustic villages, venerable Canary pines and wizened junipers. These were but a few of the island's unpublicized treasures. And where else would your taxi driver buy *you* lunch? Still little touched by tourism, El Hierro is by far the friendliest place in the Canaries.

If you want a holiday with razzmatazz, head for one of the 'big four' (with the appropriate *Landscapes* guide). But if you don't mind unrushed service, and if you want to return home more relaxed than when you left, then start packing. Discover La Gomera with *Landscapes of Southern Tenerife and La Gomera*, or use this book to enjoy the best of La Palma and El Hierro.

Acknowledgements

Special thanks to the following people for their invaluable help: Conny Spelbrink, who lives on La Palma and has completely revised this edition; the Oficina de Turismo, El Hierro; Medio Ambiente, La Palma and El Hierro; my sister Sharon, for her illustrations of island flora.

Recommended reading

There are several guides in English for both islands: you'll find the widest selection in souvenir- and bookshops on the islands themselves. For a wonderful guide to wild flowers and the local vegetation, try to buy a copy of Bramwell's *Wild flowers of the Canary Islands* on the islands, or look for it in your library.

Useful websites

www.visitlapalma.com (La Palma Tourist Board)
www.senderosdelapalma.com (official website of the island's marked trails, with updates on any closures)
www.lapalma.es (general)
www.turismodecanarias.com (official website of the Canary Islands)
www.elhierro.es (El Hierro Tourist Board)
www.iac.es (observatory website; see photo caption on page 18)
www.ecoturismocanarias.com (country cottages to rent)
See also page 134 for flight and ferry websites.

Walk 10: Ascending Pico Bejenado, near the Mirador El Rodeo

✿ Picnicking

La Palma and El Hierro are rugged and unspoilt, ideal for picnicking. On the following pages I have listed a few of my favourite picnic spots along the routes of the walks. All the information you need to get there is given on the following pages, where *picnic numbers correspond to walk numbers*. Thus you can quickly find the general location on the islands by referring to the touring maps, where the walks are numbered in green. I give transport details (🚗: car parking; 🚌: how to get there by bus), walking times, and views or setting. Beside the picnic title, you will find a map reference: the location of the picnic spot is pinpointed on this *walking map* with the symbol **P**. All of the picnic places are illustrated.

Most of these picnic spots are reached after a very short, easy walk. In fact, they make *excellent rambles for 'non-walkers'*, and are ideal for stretching your legs during car tours. Do, however, look over the comments before setting out: if some walking is involved, remember to wear sensible shoes. Always take a **sunhat** with you (○ indicates a picnic in full sun). It's a good idea to take along a plastic sheet as well, in case the ground is damp or prickly.

All picnickers should read the Country code on page 38 and go quietly in the countryside.

La Palma

1 MIRADOR LA TOSCA (map page 44, photograph page 43)

by car: 15-25min on foot	*by bus: 20-30min on foot*

🚗 Park on the concrete lane about 0.5km east of the Mirador La Tosca (Car tour 1).

🚌 bus to the Mirador La Tosca (Línea 2)

Follow the beginning of Walk 1, down to a magnificent panorama over La Tosca and the distant sea-cliffs. Dragon trees galore; shade nearby.

3 LOS TILOS (map page 48, photographs pages 50, 51) 🛋

by car: 5-30min on foot	*by bus: not easily accessible*

🚗 Park at Los Tilos car park (Car tour 1).

Below the car park there is an organised picnic area — quiet except for weekends. But I prefer picnicking below it, alongside the watercourse (canal). To get there, refer to the notes in Walk 3, from the 1h45min-point. It's an excellent spot to explore. Then perhaps refer to Short walk 3-2 to explore the fascinating barranco (which I find too busy with walking traffic for an enjoyable picnic).

6 ERMITA DE LA VIRGEN DEL PINO (map page 63)

by car: 5-20min on foot   *by bus: not easily accessible*

🚗 Park in the car park at the chapel: take the LP302 for 'Parque Nacional'; the first right turn leads to the *ermita*. (Car tour 2)
Picnic in the forest of venerable Canary pines behind the chapel.

7a LA PARED VIEJA (map pages 68-69) 🏕

by car: up to 5min on foot   *by bus: not easily accessible*

🚗 Park at the picnic area. Turn left off the El Pilar/San Isidro road just under 5km northeast of the Refugio El Pilar (signposted). (Car tour 2)
An official picnic site in a dense laurel forest. Popular on weekends.

7b (REFUGIO) EL PILAR (map pages 68-69, photo page 80) 🏕

by car: up to 5min on foot   *by bus: not easily accessible*

🚗 Park at the picnic area, off the El Pilar road (LP301), 7km south of the LP3 (Car tour 2).
An official picnic site in the woods at the foot of Pico Birigoyo. Children's playground, visitors' centre, etc. Very busy on weekends and in the summer

7c LLANO DEL JABLE (map pages 68-69, photograph page 67)

by car: up to 5min on foot   *by bus: not easily accessible*

🚗 Park under the pines: turn right off the El Pilar road onto a gravel track just beyond Montaña Quemada, 4km south of the LP3 (a detour on Car tour 2).
Picnic under pines in this 'desert' of black lapilli. Avoid on windy days.

11 CALDERA DE TABURIENTE (map pages 88-89, photograph of the *barranco* opposite) ○

by car: 20-40min on foot

🚗 Park in the bed of the Barranco de las Angustias (Car tour 3).
Picnic anywhere along the barranco. *Some 20min upstream, you will find water in the river bed. There is some shade from the ravine walls about 40min upstream, by a small cascade and pool.*

Some recommended organised picnic sites on La Palma

LAGUNA DE BARLOVENTO (map page 44; Car tour 1) △✕🏕

🚗 Park at the picnic site. Follow the LP109 southwest from Barlovento for 2km, then fork left to the picnic area.
Official site with full facilities, plus restaurant, camp ground.

EL FAYAL (map page 106; Car tour 3) 🏕

🚗 Park at the site: turn left off the LP1 (signposted for Puntagorda) 1.5km north of the main Puntagorda turn-off (the turn-off to the picnic site is also the rear entrance to the village.
Located amidst pines and tree heather; full facilities.

MONTE BREÑA (touring map; Car tour 2) 🏕

🚗 Park at the site, off the LP202 south of San José.
An official site with full facilities.

El Hierro

18a MIRADOR DE JINAMA (map pages 116-117, photo page 118)

by car: 5-15min on foot   *by bus: 10-25min on foot*

🚗 Park at the *mirador* (Car tour 4).
Picnic on the hillside above the mirador, *in the shade of pines. Or follow the path down towards Frontera for ten minutes, where you will find a belvedere*

with stone tables and benches (but no shade). There are stunning views here, but the return is steep.

18b ERMITA VIRGEN DE LA PEÑA (map pages 116-117, photographs below and page 120) ○

by car: 20-30min on foot   *by bus: 20-30min on foot*

🚗 Park at the Mirador de la Peña and walk up to the *ermita* (Car tour 4).

🚐 Guarazoca bus (Ruta 5) to the end of the route

Picnic overlooking El Golfo, alongside the chapel or along the path that descends to the sea, which is a minute above the chapel. One of the finest views in the archipelago, but very little shade.

20 MIRADOR DE LA LLANIA (map page 122, photo page 123)

by car: 5-10min on foot   *by bus: 5-10min on foot*

🚗 Park off the HI1, by the road to the Ermita de la Virgen de los Reyes (Car tour 4).

Follow the sign for the mirador *and climb to the rim of the* cumbre, *for more stunning views over the crater. Use the notes for Walk 19 to see the exquisite wooded paths in the area. Plenty of shade nearby.*

Below Dos Aguas in the Barranco de las Angustias (some two hours from the car park); the setting for Picnic 11 is similar.

21 MIRADOR DE LAS PLAYAS (map pages 128-129, similar photo page 126)

by car: up to 5min on foot   *by bus: 20-30min on foot*

🚗 Park at the the *mirador:* the turn-off lies south of San Andrés, 5km down the El Pinar/La Restinga road (Car tour 4).

🚌 Ruta 2: alight at the turn-off to the *mirador*, 700m away.

Picnic near the mirador, *with its superb coastal view. Shade of pines.*

Some recommended organised picnic sites on El Hierro

LAS PLAYAS (see touring map) 🍽

🚗 Park off the HI30 at Las Playas, 1.5km north of the *parador*.
An organised site with a spectacular backdrop.

TIMIJIRAQUE (see touring map) 🍽

🚗 Park at the site, off the HI30 south of Puerto de la Estaca
Located at one of the few sandy beaches on the island.

HOYA DEL MORCILLO (see touring map) 🍽

🚗 Park at the picnic area, described in Car tour 4, page 33.

CALA DE TACORON (see touring map) 🍽

🚗 Park at Cala de Tacorón, described in Car tour 4, page 33.

HOYA DEL PINO (see touring map) 🍽

🚗 Park at the site, off the HI1, southwest of Frontera
Surrounded by laurel forest

CHARCO MANSO (see touring map) 🍽

🚗 Park at Charco Manso, a detour on Car tour 4
Delightful sea pools, fireplaces and other facilities

LA MACETA (map pages 116-117) 🍽

🚗 Park at La Maceta, north of Frontera
Good facilities; barbecues and pools

PLAYA DEL VERODAL (see touring map) 🍽

🚗 Park at Playa del Verodal, described in Car tour 4, page 30.

PUERTO DE ORCHILLA (see touring map) 🍽

🚗 Park at Puerto de Orchilla, a detour on Car tour 4; see page 30.

The Ermita Virgen de la Peña (Picnic 18b, Walk 18)

☀ *Touring*

The **public transport** network on La Palma is quite good and, by referring to the timetables on pages 131-133, you can plan some inexpensive touring itineraries. But on El Hierro there are very few bus lines, despite recently increased services. Touring by **taxi** is another option, although a bit expensive. **Coach tours** operate on both islands (details from your hotel or the tourist offices).

Hiring your own transport is recommended on El Hierro and the most convenient way to tour La Palma as well. Car hire is relatively inexpensive, and full insurance is mostly included. Ask to see all the rental and insurance conditions (in English), and make sure you understand them. Carry the rental firm's telephone number (and a number where they can be reached outside office hours) with you. If you pay by credit card, remember to check the amount you sign for and keep all receipts!

The touring notes are brief: they include little history or other information that you can obtain in general guides or free from the local tourist offices. Instead, I've concentrated on the 'logistics' of touring: times and distances, road conditions, and seeing parts of the islands that many tourists miss. Most of all, I emphasise possibilities for **walking** and **picnicking** (the symbol *P* is used to alert you to a picnic spot; see pages 7-10). While some of the picnic and short walk suggestions may not be suitable during a long car tour, you may see a landscape that you would like to explore at leisure another day.

Most major **petrol stations** are open on Sundays and holidays, but a few of the smaller ones may not be. Take along **warm clothing** and some **food and drink**; be prepared for delays on the small country roads and tracks, and remember that mountain roads may sometimes be **impassable** in stormy weather. **Allow enough time**: the estimated driving times for each tour only includes brief stops at viewpoints labelled ☜.

The touring maps are designed to be held out facing the touring notes and contain all the information you need to follow the tours. But take time to look at the walking maps, too, when touring; they cover most of the islands in greater detail. The **symbols** in the text correspond to those on the touring maps: see map key.

11

Car tour 1: LA PALMA'S VERDANT NORTH AND THE ISLAND'S SUMMITS

Santa Cruz • Los Sauces • Barlovento • Garafía • Roque de los Muchachos • Santa Cruz

189km/117mi; 7h driving; take the northern exit from Santa Cruz.

On route: ⊼ at Los Tilos, Laguna de Barlovento; Picnics (see pages 7-10) 1, 3; Walks 1-6, 15, 16

The roads are generally very winding and, on a few stretches, narrow; some are country lanes, others might prove vertiginous for some motorists. This drive is not recommended immediately after heavy rainfall (especially in winter), due to the danger of rockfall. Where the road climbs above 600m, there's always the possibility of cloud. There is only one petrol station between Los Sauces and Santa Cruz — at the turn off for San Antonio del Monte, just after La Zarza (92km on the touring route via the observatory). Be alert for ongoing roadworks in the north, also for livestock and pedestrians on all roads: drive slowly.

Opening hours

Los Tilos Interpretation Centre free admission; daily from 09.00-14.00 and 14.30-18.25; tel 922 451246

Parque Cultural La Zarza admission €2, children half price; daily from 11.00-17.00, closed Mondays; tel 922 695005

Observatorio Astrofísico open to the public on a few days in summer: entry (2014) €9; book through the observatory's website: www.iac.es.

G aping, deep *barrancos* leave you in awe as you edge along the island's high sea shelf. The further north you go, the more desolate the landscape. Then, heading

Spring and shrine to St John the Baptist at Puntallana

inland, you climb to the rim of the crater, up through forest, to a moonscape of volcanic hues and unsurpassed panoramic views. It will be a long day, so take plenty of snacks … and don't forget your camera.

Heading north on the LP1 out of Santa Cruz, climb to the island's midriff (🚰 at 7.5km). At **Puntallana** (10km ⚡⊕) fork right into the village and, just before the church of St John the Baptist, descend a steep narrow lane to the right. Park 0.2km downhill, off the road, just before a T-junction. Traditional Canarian houses line the lane. Ivy and other creepers cascade down the ravine walls. Walk downhill a minute, then take the first right turn, to find a splendid little *plaza* shaded by a jacaranda tree, hidden in the *barranco* wall. A spring flows into small pools here, alongside a shrine to St John the Baptist.

Return to the LP1 and continue north, heading in and out of sheer-sided ravines and a series of tunnels. Less than 1km beyond **La Galga** (17km ✕), approaching a bend in the road, turn off right for the signposted **Mirador de San Bartolomé** (📷), passing the church of the same name (⚡) as you climb the hill. From this *mirador* there is a fine view inland, across the mountainous eastern wall that flanks the crater. Los Sauces is the settlement further north.

Returning to the LP1, stop at the church of San Bartolomé for a slightly unnerving cliff-edge view into the **Barranco de la Galga** (📷), then return to the main road and turn right. The track forking left just before the second tunnel is the setting for Walk 5, an easy stroll up into the laurel woods. Beyond this second tunnel another spectacular *mirador* awaits you, on the opposite side of the Barranco de la Galga. The oldest Guanche remains on La Palma, dating back to the 4th century BC, were discovered in the cave-like rock overhang you can see in the next big ravine, the **Barranco de San Juan**. The finds from this cave are exhibited in the museum at the San Francisco Convent in Santa Cruz.

At **Las Lomadas** (26.5km ✕) you reach a roundabout. Going straight ahead would take you to one of the most modern arched bridges in the world, a spectacular span 150m/500ft above the *barranco* bed (★). To the left is the turn-off for Los Nacientes (springs) de Marcos y Cordero — the first 8km on tarmac, then a rough track only suitable and only permitted for four-wheel-drive vehicles. (Alternative walk 4 ends here, emerging from the canyon that hides these mountain springs: if you're adventurous, fit and have a head for heights, make some version of Walk 4 a priority.) But for this tour, take the *next* left turn off the roundabout, for Los Tilos, and drive up another gaping *barranco,* the Barranco del Agua.

This immense dark ravine (see photograph page 47) boasts a magnificent jungle-thick laurel forest; there is also a colony of prehistoric *Woodwardia radicans* (ferns) on the gorge wall. You can learn more about La Palma's flora at the very basic visitor centre at **Los Tilos** ★ (30km *i* ✕ ⛱; *P*3), and read more about this area on pages 45-51 (Walks 3 and 4).

Leaving the Barranco del Agua, continue north on the LP1 to La Palma's third largest town, **Los Sauces** (32km ✝ ⬧ ✕ 🚰 ⊕), where Walk 2 begins and Walk 3 ends. This very pleasant (and principal) agricultural centre is swallowed up amidst banana groves. Some 1.5km out of town, branch off seaward for San Andrés (signposted). Descending through banana groves, you pass the signposted turn-off for Puerto Espíndola and Charco Azul, your route on the way back.

San Andrés (36km ✝ ⬧ ✕) sits on the hillside just above the sea. The restaurant in the square opposite the church serves good fresh fish. Wander along the cobbled lanes of the village, then peek inside the 17th-century church in the

Piscinas de la Fajana

palm-graced *plaza*, to see some rather macabre wax models. These represent ailing or injured parts of the body. In a practice dating back to the Middle Ages, they are pinned to a board on the church wall, in the hope that illnesses will be cured and injuries mended.

Return to the Puerto Espíndola junction and turn right; 0.5km further on, fork right again for the Charco Azul. Some 0.3km down this narrow lane, come to a parking bay overlooking this emerald-green natural rock-pool *(charco)*, set at the foot of low sea cliffs. *(Remember, however: when the seas are high, it's too dangerous even to venture down onto the rock here.)* Continuing on through banana groves, reach a junction and turn right into the new port of **Puerto Espíndola** (39.5km ✕), with an excellent restaurant, 'Meson del Mar'.

Ascending to the LP1, keep right. Just over 2km north along the LP1 turn right for 'Faro de Punta Cumplida'. This narrow, winding and bumpy road will take you down to some more rock pools. Keep right at the T-junction; 1.2km down, at **Punta Talavera**, there's an inconspicuous little port concealed in a rocky promontory. Park above it and walk down to the fishermen's huts that snuggle below, and to the tunnel in the rock — a very scenic spot. Swimming is only safe here when the sea is calm. After passing the **Faro de Punta Cumplida**, you climb through extensive banana plantations to a T-junction, where you turn right and descend (📷) to the **Piscinas de la Fajana** (50km ▲✕△). The pools here, larger than those at the Charco Azul, are also set in the seashore lava and are equally dangerous when the sea is high. The restaurant next to the pools has a good selection of fish and seafood, and the terrace setting is spectacular, overlooking the wild cliffs of the north coast. Walking beyond the apartments for 10 minutes, you will find some unfrequented natural pools set in a flat tongue of rough lava.

To rejoin the LP1, pass the turn-off left back to the lighthouse and keep straight uphill, ignoring all turn-offs. Turn right on the LP1 and climb to **Barlovento** (57.5km

♣✖️🚐⊕), an exposed, windswept village with a thorough-fare the width of a motorway. Walk 2 ends here. Pass the LP1 right to Gallegos and continue straight ahead for 1km, *past* the Hotel La Palma Romantica (58.5km ⛰). When you come to La Pradera (59.5km ✖️), a large prettified shed standing amidst trees off to the right, you may wish to 'go native': this popular local restaurant is a brilliant lunch or snack stop. Try the excellent grilled cheese with *mojo* sauce and a glass of red wine. Just past the restaurant, take the turn-off left to the **Laguna de Barlovento** *zona recreativa* (🚐✖️), laid out at the side of the island's largest reservoir, with a restaurant and duck pond. All sorts of birds gather in this area around the reservoir, and in the winter one can see many migrating birds as well.

Turn back from the picnic grounds and retrace your route for 3km, then fork left on the LP1 for Gallegos/Franceses. Less than 1.5km further on is the **Mirador La Tosca** (65.5km 📷*P1*), from where you have a superb view over La Tosca's dragon trees and along the wild north coast. Settlements are few and far between. Grazing is the main means of livelihood in this far-flung corner of the island. Walk 1, which starts from here, gives you a taste of this pastoral corner of the north.

Possible detours: The main tour passes above two precious little villages, Gallegos and Franceses. But I highly recommend taking detours to them if you have the time: 2km for Gallegos and just over 5km for Franceses.

Note that some of the roads are narrow and, in Franceses, some stretches of road are *vertiginous*. To make for Gallegos, where Walk 1 ends, turn right at 71.5km. Keep right on entering the village, turn sharp left in the village centre (the first left turn you come to), ignore a road to the right, and climb back up to the LP1. The flimsy sign announcing the Franceses turn-off (75km) comes up without warning. *This detour is recommended for confident drivers only.* It's a spectacular and rugged corner of the island, and relatively unvisited ... so far! You'll pass various tiny *barrios* (parts of the village), each of them named. First you squeeze through Los Machines. Then, winding in and out of gullies, ignore a turn-off to La Fajana (although it is only 2.5km off the LP1, this very narrow road down to the coast is brilliant but pretty hair-raising!). Less than 1km further on, you round a bend at the edge of the enormous Barranco Traviesa and come upon a magnificent vista across the coastal hills of the northwest. Then a steep climb takes you back up to the LP1, where you turn right.

The road snakes up through tree heather to 1100m/3600ft. Keep straight on, where the LP109 joins from the left. If you're ready for lunch, try the simple Bar/Restaurant Los Reyes in the tiny hamlet of **Roque del Faro**, 1.5km along. On cold days try the warming rabbit or goat stews, the broth, or the very tasty *gofio* dish (made from roasted maize). Wash it down with the wine called 'tea'. A great place, and as yet few tourists know about it. A slightly more sophisticated restaurant lies 4km further along: Restaurante La Mata.

Within the next 5km you reach the **Parque Cultural La Zarza**★ (90km). The small well-equipped museum here (with explanations in English) is well worth a stop. A waymarked path (allow 15-20 minutes each way) heads off behind the museum to two 'caves' (La Zarza and La Zarcita, really

The Roque de los Muchachos, at 2426m/7960ft, is La Palma's highest peak.
One of the paths from the car park leads to a nose of rock that juts out into the crater. Magnificent sweeping views await you, over the crater walls, the island's summits, and to El Hierro, La Gomera and Tenerife. Try to enjoy a sunset up here.

The Observatorio Astrofísico, near the Roque de los Muchachos, is the most important in the northern hemisphere. For fascinating details and information about visiting (in English), log on to www.iac.es.

rock overhangs), with curious Guanche petroglyphs. The meaning of these spiralled rock carvings has still not been discovered, but it is thought that they have to do with water. **Note** that there is a petrol station 1km past this point, opposite the turn-off to the houses and chapel of San Antonio del Monte.

Continuing west, when you reach the Puntagorda/ Garafía junction (⊕ Cruz Roja), turn right. Notice the old *gofio* mill on the right here. A convoluted road (LP112) down through almond groves brings you to **Garafía** (100.5km ⚕✗⊕), another isolated farming outpost, best known for breeding livestock. Reaching the village, turn right for the 16th-century church of Nuestra Señora de la Luz★, one of the largest on the island. It has an interesting wooden ceiling. Walk 16 begins and ends here … but the truth is that few hikers venture out this far into the 'sticks'. For food there are two local restaurants here, both offering good, plain cooking in simple surroundings: Santo Domingo in the *plaza* and La Taberna Santi next to the supermarket.

Leaving Garafía, you can make a pleasant circuit by continuing past the square and taking the first right. Then turn right again, to return to the main road. Making for Las Tricias, turn right and follow the road south. Another *gofio* (maize) mill appears on the right as you leave Garafía. Once again settlement is sparse. Two more impressive ravines are crossed. Climbing slopes clad with almond trees, you pass through picturesque **Las Tricias★** (112km), a retreat for 'alternative life-stylers'. Walk 15 would take you right down amongst them all. But it's really the great clumps of dragon trees everyone comes to see (photograph page 104).

Just 1km above Las Tricias you meet the LP1 signposted back to Garafía. Turn left uphill here, to begin your ascent to the Roque de los Muchachos. After 10km branch off right on the LP4. The ascent gets steeper, the bends sharper. Stunning scenery unravels — over the farmlands

18

of the north, the thickly wooded hillsides, and the sea. Nearer the rim of the crater, the pines vanish and *codeso* (broom) carpets the ground. Pass th first observatory buildings, turn right at the first junction, and head up to the island's highest peak, the **Roque de los Muchachos**★ (145km 📷*i*).

For a spectacular view into the Caldera de Taburiente, walk down to the salient of rock on the right, behind the car park. Over the shoulder of the crater the white-domed buildings of the **Observatorio Astrofísico** glare back at you. This complex, the most important in the northern hemisphere, has 13 telescopes — two for the sun and the other 11 for the furthest galaxies. The Gran Telescopio Canario (installed in 2007) is one of the largest telescopes in the world.

Return to the junction with the LP4 and turn right for Santa Cruz. Rounding the *caldera*, the deep volcanic yellows, oranges and reds in the rock distract you from the panoramic views. Two more *miradors* (**Los Ándenes** and **Degollada de Franceses**) on the very edge of the crater (📷) give you another chance to take in this great work of nature. Descending, re-enter the pine zone and after 8km pass the Pico de la Nieve track, starting point for Walk 6 and Short walk 6. Over the pines the east coast begins to open up and, lower down, you get a fine view of Santa Cruz, with a prominent half-crater backdrop. On reaching the LP401, keep left, then turn right on the LP1 into **Santa Cruz** (189km).

Car tour 2: VOLCANIC SPLENDOURS IN THE SOUTH OF LA PALMA

Santa Cruz • Los Canarios (Fuencaliente) • El Paso • El Pilar • Santuario de las Nieves • Santa Cruz

134km/84mi; 5h driving; take the southern exit from Santa Cruz

On route: ⊼ at Las Toscas (Mazo), on the main road above Las Indias, Refugio El Pilar, La Pared Vieja; Picnics (see pages 7-10) 6, 7a-b, (7c); Walks 6-9, (10)

Driving will be slow, due to narrow winding roads. The southern tip of the island can be very windy.

Opening hours
Mazo, market days: 15.00-19.00 Sat; 09.00-13.00 Sun
El Molino (ceramics centre): 09.00-17.00 Mon-Fri, except during lunch hours (13.00-15.00)
Cueva de Belmaco (archaeological museum) 10.00-18.00 (Mon-Sat), 10.00-15.00 (Sun)
Bodegas Llanovid: 08.00-14.00 and 15.00-17.00 Mon-Fri
National Park Visitor Centre: 09.00-18.30 daily, including holidays

You'll marvel at the volcanic landscapes on this tour, the kaleidoscope of scenery, and the striking colour contrasts. Gastronomic delights, plain but hearty, lie on route as well — indulge yourself.

Head south on the LP2, passing the long man-made Playa de Bajamar. The turn-off right to the Playa de los Cancajos (▲▲▲✕) lies 3km along: with its rock-studded coves, it is the best beach in the vicinity. Just 0.1km further on, turn right (Exit 2b) and, at a roundabout follow signposting for Los Canarios. Beyond the airport turn-off, you head through colourful **San Antonio** (4.5km ▲✕). Some 1.5km further on, you come to a junction. The main tour continues to the right here, up into the hills (LP206, signposted to San José). But if you are interested in the history of the island, I'd suggest the lower route (LP2 signposted to Los Canarios). This runs via El Hoyo de Mazo (10km ✕). Souvenir hunters may enjoy El Molino, the hillside windmill and ceramics shop on the outskirts of El Hoyo (11km), which was originally an ironmongery. It is beautifully kept, and in spring the garden is an extravaganza of colour. The artisans here specialise in replicas of the Guanche era. Further on you would pass the Cueva de Belmaco★ (15.5km ⌒M), a large overhang of rock by the roadside with a small archaeological museum. Four rocks on the edge of the overhang are engraved with still-undeciphered petroglyphs.

Continuing the main tour uphill on the LP206, keep left at both the major junctions you encounter and ignore any turn-offs. The garden plots disappear and the hillsides are overgrown. Entering **Mazo** (12km ⭢▲✕⊕ and Las

Toscas 🎋), take the upper road. The market and handicraft centre here are popular with tourists, as is the Corpus Christi festival in June, when flower petals are laid in the streets as pictures and carpets. Mazo, like El Hoyo de Mazo, is a wine-producing area, well known for its strong red wine. Alternative Walk 7 ends here.

Beyond **Tigalate** (19km), the historians and shoppers rejoin the route at the Mazo/Los Canarios junction. The LP2 takes you across a jagged lava stream, dating from the 1646 eruption of Volcán San Martín (Walk 9). At the 25km-mark a track signposted 'Pino de la Virgen' turns off right to the Fuente de los Roques *zona recreativa*.

Soon the change in scenery is spectacular. Volcanoes begin appearing on the southern tip of the island, where eruptions have dramatically transformed the landscape. Pines are liberally dispersed across the lava, which is covered in reindeer moss. The *cumbre* falls into the sea. Entering the wine-producing village of **Los Canarios** (also known as Fuencaliente; 28km ♠✕➡⊕), where Walk 9 ends and Walk 8 begins, you pass the turn-offs for both the lighthouse (Faro de Fuencaliente) and the volcanoes. The village, the highest on the island, sits on the tail of the *cumbre*, at 680m/2230ft. If you're ready for coffee, try the almond cakes in the Bar La Parada, along to the right.

Return to the first junction in the village and turn right for Las Indias and the volcanoes of San Antonio and Teneguía. This is one of the best grape-growing areas in the Canaries, and soon you will see the large Bodega Teneguía (✕) on your right. It's known for its extensive selection of wines, the most famous being the well-known *malvasia* (malmsey), which has won several international prizes.

Descending into the volcanic world that is the setting for Walk 8, weird and wonderful sights await you. Less than 1km downhill, turn left to the signposted **Volcán de San Antonio★** (29.5km). The entrance fee of €5 covers parking and access to the volcano (📷) and visitors' centre (*i*). Thought to be at least 3200 years old, the volcano last erupted in 1677. (See Walk 8 on page 73 to reach **Roque Teneguía** and the **Volcán de Teneguía★** from here.)

Continuing towards Las Indias, you have a fine view (📷) onto yellow Roque Teneguía, once a sacred rock, covered with petroglyphs, with the rich blue sea behind it. The jet-black inclines are splashed with lime-green grape vines. Banana plantations lie along the sea flat amidst the lava flows. The village of Los Quemados sits on a pause in the hillside below. Ignore turn-offs to the left. Descending through the sprawling hillside village of **Las Indias** (33km), you look across the southern slopes onto Puerto Naos, with the wall of the *caldera* behind it. At a T-junction with signs for 'La Zamora' and 'El Faro', turn left. (Or first take a 3km return detour to the *right*, to the pretty little cove of Playa de Zamora. Some 200m past the signposted lane down to the parking area for the *kiosko*, you'll see a path descending to Playa de Zamora, a cove set at the foot of high cliffs. Please don't sit directly below the cliffs, as there is often rockfall. Several rocky islets sit offshore, and the coastline has pinkish cliffs. Just above Playa de Zamora is one of the few *kioskos* left on the coast, serving up good fish and great views (many of these 'sheds', some illegally built, but all full of 'local colour', were closed down by the authorities in recent years).

Turning left at the bottom of the road, you weave in and out of banana plantations and pass an impressive hotel complex (▲▲). A pretty inlet follows just over 2km further on. Then a track turns off to the right, to Punta Larga. Out of the banana groves, you head through old and newer lava flows. The newer flow was caused by Teneguía in 1971 and embraces the pretty beach of Playa Echentive (or Playa Nueva; 43.5km). Some 1km further on, turn right for 'El Faro'. Keep right at the fork. (The left fork would take you to some tiny unfrequented coves hidden in the shoreline, worth a visit one day.) **Faro de Fuencaliente** (46.5km; photographs pages 76-77), the out-of-the-way fishermen's retreat where Walk 8 ends, is well worth the visit. There is a small but interesting maritime visitors' centre in the old lighthouse. This is also a good  swimming spot, except when a strong south or southwesterly wind is blowing. The public may enter the salt pans here, but you must keep to the walkways. Right in the middle of the salt pans is a new themed restaurant, 'Jardin de la Sal' (✗), with excellent views and equally great food. Salt from the *salinas* can be bought in a little shop next to it.

Return to the road and turn right. The deep red-tinted Volcán de Teneguía catches your attention as you ascend into volcanic mounds. Climb steeply through

The Volcán de Teneguía: in summer the nearby vineyards are a blaze of brightness in this sombre and windswept landscape.

the fresh lava streams of Teneguía and pass through the apron of vineyards that encircle the village of Los Canarios (57km). Back on the LP2, turn left, go through the village and soon pass two roadside picnic areas (⊼) overlooking the coast — one to the right and one to the left. Half a kilometre past the second picnic area lies the **Mirador de las Indias** (📷), from where you have an excellent view back over terraced vineyards and the village of the same name. The road climbs to 800m/2625ft, with marvellous sea views. At 64km **El Charco**, another *mirador* (📷), affords fine views across the cliffs, over to Puerto Naos. Beyond a shady pine wood, you overlook great spewings of lava from eruptions in the 18th century. The picturesque village of **Jedey** sits amidst this turmoil. **Las Manchas**, an area of viticulture, follows. Then you come to one of the most popular bodegas on the island, Bodegón/Restaurant Tamanca (72km ✕), a cave cut into the hillside. At the very least try some cheese and ham with a tipple! You'll see the mounted head of a *mouflon* (barbary sheep) in the bar: a few still roam the heights of the *caldera*.

The village of **San Nicolás** lies just around the bend. During the volcanic eruption of 1949, San Nicolás was in the path of a descending lava flow. The people prayed together to save their village, and the flow changed course. It encircled the village, but then continued below it. A shrine commemorates this miracle.

Remain on the LP2 beyond San Nicolás. Settlement slowly creeps over the sloping plain. On reaching the Los Canarios/Los Llanos junction, at **Tajuya** (76km ✕), turn

Santa Cruz from the Mirador de la Concepción. Stepping up the sheer cumbre, *the town is very photogenic from this hilltop.*

right uphill on the LP3 to El Paso. The towering crater walls are the focal point in the landscape. **El Paso** (79km ♈♠▲✕⛽⊕) sprawls amidst the gardens, orchards, and almond fields that cover the floor of a high open valley. This village is a favourite with expatriates.

Some 3km above El Paso, at the second roundabout, turn left on the LP302 for the Parque Nacional. Stop at the parking area on the right for the National Park Information Centre (*i*), to pick up a free admission ticket for your next stop, the Cumbrecita (no ticket is needed after 15.00). Pass through the first junction (where a right turn leads to the Ermita de la Virgen del Pino and a grand pine; *P*6, Walk 6), then keep right at the next junction for La Cumbrecita. (Keeping straight on here would take you to the starting point for Walk 10 which climbs Pico Bejenado.) From **La Cumbrecita** (89km 📷) you enjoy a splendid view over the Caldera de Taburiente, a massive cauldron filled with jagged blades of tumbling ridges.

Return to the LP3 and turn left. After 3km turn right on the LP301 for the El Pilar Zona Recreativa and climb steadily, in an appealing landscape of coal-black slopes and pine forest. You pass a track off right 4km uphill: it leads to the small volcanic 'desert' shown on page 67, the **Llano del Jable** (📷*P*7c, Walk 7). About 1km further on, where a track heads south is the eponymous *mirador,* with fine views over the volcanic plains you just passed and up to Los Llanos in the distance. Just before crossing the *cumbre,* you pass the **Refugio El Pilar** (106km △🅿*P*7b, Walks 6, 7 and 9), a popular picnic and camping area in a pine forest. Just above it, to the left, is the Cumbre Nueva track that is followed in Alternative walk 6-1.

On the other side of the *cumbre* the vegetation changes from pines to heather. A dark green carpet of dense woods stretches across the eastern escarpment. This fine view reaches as far as Puntallana. On clear days El Teide can be seen above the foaming white clouds that separate La Palma and Tenerife (☎ at 109km). Some 1.5km below the viewpoint lies **La Pared Vieja** (⌂*P*7a, Walk 7), a picnic area in laurel woods.

Returning to civilization, you enter the farming village of **San Isidro** (118km), which enjoys an expansive panorama along the wall of the *cumbre* and over the twin villages of San Pedro and San José. San Isidro is known for its cattle market, held in May. Continuing downhill, soon you'll spot a large dragon tree below the road, off a sharp bend — actually two trees, intertwined (**Los Dragos Gemelos★**; the 'twins'). Reaching the LP202, head left into **San Pedro** (also known as Breña Alta; 123km ▲✕🍴) in the midst of a tobacco-growing area. A farmer's market is held here each Saturday morning. Circle the *plaza*, remaining on the LP202. At the next important junction, cross over the LP3, to continue towards the 'Santuario de las Nieves'. But first turn off right at the roundabout just ahead, to the **Mirador de la Concepción** (☎), the perfect spot from which to view Santa Cruz. Back at the roundabout, the beautiful red building is the restaurant Casa Osmunda (✕), with Palmerian *'nouvelle cuisine'* — quite a novelty on the island. Keep straight on at the roundabout. You pass the restaurant Chipi Chipi, on the left. Housed in cabanas in a courtyard crammed with greenery, it is reasonably priced and always packed.

Rounding a bend, you look across a ravine sprinkled with palms to the tree-shaded **Santuario de las Nieves★** (129km ✝M), strikingly set in a rocky ridge. To reach the sanctuary, turn right at the roundabout. The church (16C) houses a 15th-century terracotta statue of the island's patron saint, Our Lady of the Snows. Her festival is celebrated annually on the fifth of August. But every five years a month-long fiesta takes place (the 'Bajada de la Virgen'), when the statue is carried down into Santa Cruz. It draws tens of thousands of pilgrims and tourists.

Drive down from the church back onto the LP101 and, following signs for Santa Cruz, take the second turning to the right. A very steep, winding descent takes you back to **Santa Cruz** far below (134km).

Los Llanos • Caldera de Taburiente • Barranco de las Angustias • Los Brecitos • Tazacorte • Mirador El Time • (Puntagorda) • Los Llanos

57km/36mi; 3-4h driving. See also large-scale map on pages 88-89.

On route: Picnic (see pages 7-10) 11; Walks 11, 12. (Walks 13 and 14 and the El Fayal picnic site (⚞) are on the Puntagorda detour route.)

Drive carefully: although the road up to Los Brecitos is now tarmac, it is very narrow and vertiginous. Parking is not allowed at Los Brecitos, and you may be turned back by a park warden if there are too many cars on the road. The best solution is to drive only as far as the Barranco de las Angustias, the floor of the crater, and then take one of the shuttle jeep or van taxis up to Los Brecitos (these only operate from 08.30 until about 12.30); the shared cost is about € 12-13.

All visitors to La Palma should spend at least one day in the magnificent Caldera de Taburiente. This short tour is designed to be combined with Short walk 11, as a half-day tour, half-day hike.

Leaving from **Los Llanos** (🛉🏔🔺✕🖵⊕), turn north on Avenida Doctor Fleming and turn right at the T-junction. The road curves round to the left: go through an intersection and follow signs for 'La Caldera', keeping right at the first fork and left at the second. Climb to the edge of the Barranco de las Angustias and, at a T-junction, turn right to descend into the **Caldera de Taburiente★**.

Some 5km along you're in the bed of the dramatic **Barranco de las Angustias** (*P*11). If there are not too many tourists about, and the park wardens don't turn you back, you may be able to take your car further up the road. Otherwise I highly recommend sharing a jeep taxi up to **Los Brecitos** (16km 🚐). Whether with your own wheels or by jeep taxi, the 11km climb of almost 1000m/ 3300ft, will take you through mountain scenery unequalled on the island. On your return, *do* follow at least part of Short walk 11 to make the most of your visit; see notes on page 86.

From the *caldera* retrace your route to **Los Llanos** (32km) and turn right on the main LP2. Some 2km downhill, follow the LP2 left to **Tazacorte** (39.5km 🏔🔺✕🖵⊕), buried amidst

On the drive up to Los Brecitos

26

the banana plantations that cover these slopes. Continue through the village to **Puerto de Tazacorte** (40km ⏺✕), a colourful and fashionable seaside village with lovely restaurants lining the boulevard beside the beach. From here ascend the canyon-sized Barranco de las Angustias again (photograph page 94).

Joining the LP1, continue left uphill to the **Mirador El Time** (47.5km 📷✕), the climax of one of the island's most exhilarating routes. The impressive *barranco* plunges 500m/1650ft directly below you here, and your view fans out over the banana plantations that fill the extensive Los Llanos valley, to the *cumbre*, and along the volcano-dented southern spine. Walk 12 winds its way down these sheer cliffs to Puerto de Tazacorte; it makes an excellent late afternoon walk.

Suggested detour, 32km return: If you have time, consider going on to Puntagorda via Tijarafe (✕🏪⊕) and Tinizara (✕). Tijarafe's Walk 13, which will turn your legs to jelly, is a must for the fit. Walk 14 is a gentler roller-coaster hike, from Tijarafe to Tinizara. At Puntagorda there is the El Fayal picnic site and a nearby indoor market selling local foods and handicrafts (weekends only)

Otherwise, pour yourself a glass of the local wine, put your feet up, and take in an 'El Time sunset', before heading back the 9.5km along the LP1 to **Los Llanos** (57km).

Car tour 4: EL HIERRO — HIGHLIGHTS

Tigaday • Sabinosa • La Dehesa • (Faro de Orchilla) • Cruz de los Reyes • Hoya del Morcillo • El Pinar • Cala de Tacorón • Mirador de las Playas • Mirador de Jinama • Mirador de la Peña • Mocanal • Pozo de las Calcosas • Valverde • San Andrés • Tigaday

184km/115mi; 5h driving; start out from Tigaday.

On route: ⟁ at Playa del Verodal, (Puerto de Orchilla), Hoya del Morcillo, Cala de Tacorón, (Charco Manso, Las Playas); Picnics (see pages 7-10) 18a-b, 19, 20; Walks 17-21

This tour follows roads of all kinds. Some 25km is on gravel (not recommended immediately after wet weather, due to rockfall). The detour to the Faro de Orchilla takes in an extra 10km of sometimes rough road (in winter or after heavy rain only suitable for four wheel drive vehicles). There are two narrow stretches of road without guard rails which some motorists may find unnerving: on the ascent up the cumbre *beyond the turn-off to Playa del Verodal, and on the road to the Cala de Tacorón in the south. Note that visibility on the* cumbre *can be zero, due to low clouds and mist. Always be alert for foraging animals. Petrol is only available at Taibique (near El Pinar), Tigaday and Valverde (some stations will be closed in the afternoon on Sundays and holidays). All the roads are generally narrow and winding, so drive slowly.*

Opening hours

Eco-museo de Guinea and Lagartario: open daily all year from 10.00-18.00, but closed on Sundays and Mondays in winter

The diversity of landscapes encountered on this tiny island will leave you spellbound. There are vast open tracts of lava, fields of craters, herbaceous highlands, spacious forests of towering pines, small boskets of laurel, and inviting rock pools. If you're rushed for time, then keep to the main tour, but if you're on the island for a few days, then *do* try to take all the suggested detours.

Tigaday is the starting point for the drive. For those of you staying elsewhere, recommended sights in the vicinity are the Eco-museo de Guinea, a restored hamlet, and the nearby Lagartario which houses the large Salmor lizards (both on the road to Las Puntas); the Embarcadero de Punta Grande (if only to see the smallest hotel in the world!); and the bell-tower of Frontera's church, which crowns a rust-red volcanic hill above the church itself. The hilltop is the perfect spot to take in a sunset.

Set out from **Frontera/Tigaday** (⚱🏔🔺⚔🚏⊕) by heading west towards Sabinosa on the HI50. You pass through a string of villages (⚔) set on the steep rocky volcanic slopes that roll down off the *cumbre*. Fig trees and vineyards grow out of the *malpais* that coats the slopes (try the fine local wine, the *vino de pata*).

Rounding a hillside, you overlook **Sabinosa** (8km 🔺⚔), the village shown on page 114. Stark and severe, this whitewashed settlement is the island's prize — superbly sited on volcanic slopes at the foot of the wooded central spine of mountains. Short walk 17-2 starts here, and Short walk 17-1 ends here. Terraced vineyards ladder the surrounding hillsides.

A narrow winding road takes you down to the health spa of **Pozo de la Salud★** (12km 🏔🔺⚔🎞), known for the reputedly curative powers of its sulphur and radium spring. This one-horse hamlet enjoys a superb backdrop. From the pretty, manicured *mirador* below the hotel you can look along the low craggy sea cliffs into a viridescent sea. Drink some of the salty spring water from the little well in the rock here, where the sheer *cumbre* walls provide a magnificent backdrop; the scenery alone has curative powers!

Continuing further west, you enter the island's most striking and isolated corner, where an extravaganza of volcanic scenery awaits you. Explore it on foot: I *highly recommend* easy Walk 19 for everyone: stop at the parking area (14.6km) for **Arenas Blancas**, a tiny patch of golden yellow sand set in the lava coastline. Disappearing into *malpais* again, stabs of rich volcanic reds and orange-tinted

Looking across Tigaday and Frontera to the wall of the El Golfo crater. The bell-tower of Frontera's church (Virgen de la Candelaria) stands apart on a rust-red hilltop. Walk 18 ascends the wooded slopes at the right-hand side of the photograph.

rust-brown hues catch your attention. Your next turn-off comes up at 17.5km: turn sharp right for 'Playa del Verodal'. Then, 100m further on, where the asphalt ends, turn right on a good track. The red sandy beach of **Playa del Verodal** (18.5km 🏖) is a pretty, but windy spot, with a dramatic backdrop of maroon-tinted cliffs. *Beware:* the sea can be rough here!

Back on the main road, turn right. Ascending steeply, superb views over the coastal lava shelf unfold behind you. The landscape is barren and rocky; xerophytic vegetation grows out of the rock. This part of the island is known as **La Dehesa**.

Suggested detour: Some 27km en route you reach the signposted turn-off right for the Faro de Orchilla. The first 2km is partly asphalted, then you turn left on a motorable track (in winter or after heavy rain only suitable for 4WD). Descending to the lighthouse, you enter a world of volcanic cones and lava streams and look down over a jagged, lava-encrusted point of land. Notice the massive *Euphorbias* growing out of the lava here. Red-tinted craters come out of hiding. Approaching the lighthouse, you pass a heavily-signposted fork leading left to tiny Puerto de Orchilla (🏖), where it's possible to swim. Up until 1844, the Faro de Orchilla★ (📷) was 'the edge of the world': before it was repositioned at Greenwich, 0° of longitude was located here at the western edge of El Hierro. Amble along the impressive sea cliffs behind the building. Then return to the main road and turn right.

The main tour bypasses the Orchilla turn-off. You drive over two cattle-grids and, at the junction that follows, turn left for the 'Mirador del Basco' and 'El Sabinar', soon coming to the **Ermita de la Virgen de los Reyes**★ (30.5km ✝; Walk 17). This dazzling-white, isolated refuge (photograph page 111) is the sanctuary of the island's patron saint. Every four years, on the first weekend in July, a very popular pilgrimage (the 'Bajada de la Virgen') begins here, and an image of the Madonna crosses the island to Valverde.* The fiesta continues for almost a month.

Half a kilometre further on the way reverts to a rutted gravel road. At a signposted junction, turn left. Another cattle-grid is encountered, and again the countryside

---

*The island's most famous walk, the 28km-long 'Camino de la Virgin', follows this pilgrimage route; a leaflet detailing the various stages is available from tourist offices. It is also shown on our walking maps, since we follow the trail from time to time.

Above: the Eco-museo de Guinea near Tigaday — a restored old village.
Right: hotel at Pozo de la Salud, with the cliffs of the cumbre *rising vertically in the background.*

changes. Undulating pastures criss-crossed with stone walls stretch back up to the hills. Remaining on the main metalled road, take the first turn-off left and wind your way down to **El Sabinar★** (34.5km), a magnificent refuge for scatterings of centuries-old, twisted and gnarled *sabinas* (native junipers) — the result of the harsh unrelenting winds that batter this corner of the island. Less than 1km downhill, the track ends just in front of the island's most famous and most photographed specimen (see page 1). An interesting information board explains the origin of these weird, 'arthritic' trees — unique in the archipelago. The surrounding vegetation here is thickly covered in moss and lichen. Please note that this is a protected area.

Return to the junction and turn left. Further north along the gravel road, you meet a fork: keep right for the *mirador,* driving through fragments of pine woods — a picturesque corner in this inhospitable area. The **Mirador del Basco** (36.5km 📷) sits high on the very edge of the escarpment that encircles El Golfo. The stunning panorama extends all across the gulf, with Pozo de la Salud immediately below you.

Returning to the junction just before the *ermita* (41km), go straight on for 'Valverde' and 'El Pinar'. A meandering ascent takes you up to the island's cloud-swept heights. Pines patch the gravelly slopes. Pass the turn-off right for El Julán and Hoya del Morcillo, and keep left, now on a gravel road. Volcanic hues of maroon, pink, and yellow stain the hillsides. High on the *cumbre,* your view stretches over the pines to the sea and then to the treeless southern tip of La Restinga. You pass below El Hierro's highest summit, Malpaso (1500m/4920ft), without even noticing it (but for the signpost).

A simple wooden cross and concrete altar by the side of the road mark **Cruz de los Reyes** (56.5km), the pilgrims' rest stop en route to Valverde from the Ermita de la Virgen de los Reyes. On a sealed road once again, you

Rock pools (charcos) *at Cala de Tacorón*

look out over the low wooded hills of El Pinar, your next destination. Coming to the Frontera/Valverde junction (starting point for Walk 21), keep right along the HI1, immediately passing the starting point for Walk 20 and the signposted path to the **Mirador de la Llanía** (☞*P*19). Some 0.4km further on, turn right for 'Hoya del Morcillo, El Pinar, La Restinga'. Briefly disappearing into laurel woods, the road winds down towards El Pinar, passing through El Hierro's majestic Canary pine wood, where centuries-old pines with massive girths leave you in awe. Just under 4km downhill, keep right. Follow this up with a left turn into the large picnic area of **Hoya del Morcillo** (64.5km △⊼), set in the middle of the forest. Return to the main road and turn right for El Pinar and La Restinga. At the T-junction that follows, turn right again. The nearby slopes are liberally sprinkled with almond trees.

Entering **El Pinar**, which comprises the villages of **Las Casas** and **Taibique**, take the first right turn (signposted 'Tanajara'), where the main road curves left. Keep straight through a junction, then turn right at the next junction and ascend a narrow road up to the **Mirador Tanajara** (69km ☞). If you're game, climb the wooden viewing platform for a good view over the sprawling villages of Las Casas and Taibique. The fields are scattered with large umbrella-shaped fig trees, and almond, apricot and pear trees abound, as do small vineyards. To the south lies a chain of volcanic craters. Back on the main road, turn right for 'El Pinar' and 'Restinga' and descend to **Taibique** (72.5km ▲▲▲✕⬛⊕M). The village is known for its handicrafts: woodcarving, basketry, and weaving.

Out of the village, you descend south through a curious landscape of ropey lava and block lava. Less than 10km below El Pinar, turn off right for Cala de Tacorón (signposted). Descending into a striking sea view across the western wing of the island, the road twists its way down a sheer slope to a lava platform jutting out into the sea. **Cala de Tacorón** (87km ⊼) is a quiet, out-of-the-way spot with superb *charcos* (sea pools) for swimmers, mouth-watering scenery, and a lovely little bar that serves food. With the south's more reliable sunshine, this is the place to come for your beach day. It beats La Restinga hands down. The main tour in fact bypasses La Restinga (▲✕), by turning left at the Tacorón junction, heading straight back to El Pinar. (La Restinga, small fishing village-cum-resort, 7km to the south, has little to offer other than good fish restaurants.)

From **El Pinar** keep straight uphill past the El Morcillo junction, then turn off right to the **Mirador de las Playas** (109.5km 📷; Walk 21). From the edge of a 1000m/ 3300ft-high bluff, you look straight down onto the severe but breathtakingly beautiful *playas* — the setting shown in the photograph on page 126.

Back on the main road, head right. The hillsides are covered in *tagasaste*, a shrub grown for animal fodder. Climbing to a tableland, you reach the roof of the island, home of the best pastures, where cows and sheep graze. San Andrés is the small village over on the right, encircling the base of a small volcanic cone (photograph page 127). When you rejoin the HI1, keep left and, 2km along, turn right to the **Mirador de Jinama** (117.5km 📷; *P*18a, Walk 18) where, from the top of the *cumbre*, your view stretches the length of El Golfo to the west.

Continuing northeast on a narrow country road, bump your way across the plateau, lost amidst the myriad of stone walls that divide it up into tiny squares. When a farmer dies on El Hierro, his fields are always divided up among all his children, each of whom partitions his or her share. And so the fields get smaller, while the walls increase. Small cinder cones cover the plateau.

You descend to the HI10, where you turn left downhill for 2km to the **Mirador de la Peña★** (124.5km 📷✕; *P*18b, Walk 18). Lanzarote's César Manrique was the creator of this superbly-sited restaurant/ bar, which claims the island's best view of El Golfo. These cliffs were the habitat of a very rare lizard, the *lagarto de salmor*, which supposedly reaches a length of 70cm/28in. (*Do* visit the Lagartario at the Eco-museo de Guinea!)

Continuing north through fertile farmlands and the hamlets of **Guarazoca** and **Erese**, dense xerophytic vegetation cloaks the rocky inclines. The traditional stone dwellings are hardly noticeable in this backdrop. Entering **Mocanal** (128km), the most picturesque village on the island, take the first turn-off left (along the old road). This narrow road squeezes past a string of charming old houses, where window and door frames all vary in colour.

Just over 1km along, at a signposted, slightly larger junction, turn left for Pozo de las Calcosas. A steep winding descent follows. The slopes ease out as they roll seawards. *Vinagrera* (of the dock family) proliferates here and provides a source of food for the many goats. ('Calcosas' is the local name for *vinagrera*.) At the next junction, go straight on for **Pozo de las Calcosas★** (133.5km

●✕☞), which at first appears to be an unexciting hamlet set back off the sea cliffs. However, on the rocky shore at the foot of these bluffs sits a century-old, once-deserted fishing hamlet which has been beautifully restored. Steps lead down to this appealing huddle of stone houses and the nearby natural rock pool. The restaurants above the *mirador* here serve excellent fresh seafood.

At the junction above Pozo de las Calcosas, turn left for **Echedo** (138.5km ✕), a wine- and fruit-producing village boasting the best climate on the island. Entering the village, ignore a turning to the right, but turn right at the T-junction that follows. (A left turn at this T-junction would take you to the brilliant blue sea pools of Charco Manso, 4km away; ⊟) Surrounded by rocky hills and scattered amidst the now-familiar stone walls, Echedo is a charmer. Ascending to Valverde, you overlook the black and brown slopes of Montaña Tanagiscaba. Meet the main road and turn left.

After just 100m you're at the **Mirador de las Pernadas** (☞), from where there is a fine view over the tiny seaside resort of Tamaduste. Then you come to a junction on the outskirts of **Valverde** (142km ✝●▲✕⊕M). This small, rather plain rural town sits at an altitude of 700m. Turn right and pass through the town.

Suggested detours: If you are on the island for a while, you may wish to visit the seaside resort of Tamaduste (●✕), 8km north of the capital via the airport road, or take the very scenic coastal route from Puerto de la Estaca (two ⊟) to the *parador* (▲▲✕), 18km southeast of Valverde.

Leave Valverde on the HI1. Bypassing Tiñor, you climb above steep, rocky, xerophyte-clad slopes to the small traditional farming village of **San Andrés** (✕). At an altitude of 1100m, this is El Hierro's highest village. (The turn-off to Isora, just before San Andrés, leads to the Mirador de Isora, another spectacular lookout point over Las Playas. Alternative walk 21 makes a fairly hair-raising descent down the sheer escarpment that tumbles away below this *mirador*.) The famous 'Arbol Santo' worshipped by the Bimbaches (El Hierro's original inhabitants) is not far from San Andrés; Walk 21 would take you to it.

Go straight through both junctions just outside San Andrés, and once again weave your way through the maze of stone walls, following the HI1 — the spectacular, but long and winding old road through the laurel forest — back to **Tigaday** (175km).

✿ Walking

La Palma and El Hierro offer unlimited scope for walkers. This book covers a good cross-section of walks on both islands. Due to the rugged, mountainous terrain of these islands, many of the walks in the book are quite strenuous, but I usually suggest a less difficult alternative — perhaps a short walk, or just a stroll to a picnic spot.

Guides, waymarking, maps

Should you wish to hire a **guide**, enquire at the tourist offices or at hotels.

Many trails on both islands are now **waymarked** and **signposted** (but that doesn't necessarily mean that they are in good condition or suitable for inexperienced walkers!). There are three main types of waymarking:

- *Red and white* waymarks indicate GR routes ('Grandes Recorridos': long-distance footpaths);
- *Yellow and white* waymarks indicate PR routes ('Pequeños Recorridos': short trails of up to six hours);
- *Green and white* waymarks indicate SL routes ('Senderos Locales': local trails, up to about 10km long).
- For all these routes, right-angled stripes indicate a 'change of direction; an 'X' means 'wrong way'.

We show the *approximate* line of these waymarked routes, with numbers, *in purple* on our walking maps. *This should give you ample scope for devising even more walks — perhaps a linear route to catch a bus or a circuit back to your car.* For full details of waymarked walks on **La Palma**, see www.senderosdelapalma.com; *this site also has downloadable* **GPS tracks** *for many routes and files for viewing in Google Earth.* For **El Hierro** see www. elhierro.es (click on tourism, then on maps); in future this site may also offer GPS tracks.

The **maps** in this book, based on Spanish military maps and reproduced at a scale of 1:50,000, cover most of both islands and have been heavily adapted and updated. If you require further maps, you should find the Freytag + Berndt maps of La Palma (1:50,000) and El Hierro (1:30,000) more useful than the older military maps.

Where to stay

There are two main resorts on **La Palma**: Los Cancajos on the eastern side of the island and Puerto Naos in the west. There is also a large Princess chain hotel in Fuencaliente near the coast. All are fairly well served by public transport. But I would recommend Santa Cruz or Los Llanos over any of these resorts, both for atmosphere and for getting to and from walks by public transport. If you have a hire car, however, the island's your oyster — and you might choose to rent one of the *casas rurales* (charming old country houses converted into tourist accommodation). They are reasonably priced and often superbly located. *I highly recommend them.* For information, contact the Asociación de Turismo Rural (tel: 922-430625) or see www.islabonita.com.

The main tourist centres on **El Hierro** are Tigaday/Frontera and La Restinga. Tigaday is my choice, but La Restinga boasts more sunshine. Although bus services on the island have increased somewhat, you really *do* need to rent a car to make the best of El Hierro.

Both La Palma and El Hierro have **government-run hotels** *(paradores)*. El Hierro's is magnificently sited (see photograph on page 126), but well off the beaten track. Independent travellers should always book their accommodation a few nights in advance — in the peak season (Christmas through Easter), at least a month in advance!

Transport
The public transport network on La Palma is good enough for you to be able to do most of the walks I describe using the local buses. However, on El Hierro, there are fewer buses, so you will often have to use a taxi or a hired car.

What to take
If you've come to the islands without special equipment, you can still do many of the walks — or you can buy the basic equipment at one of the sports shops. *Don't* attempt the more difficult walks without the proper gear. For each walk, the *minimum year-round* equipment is listed. Above all, you need strong shoes or boots with *ankle support*. You may find this checklist useful:

stout shoes or walking boots	long trousers, tight at the ankles
waterproof rain gear (outside summer months)	mobile phone
	knives and openers
long-sleeved shirt (sun protection)	fleece (or similar)
bandages and plasters, tissues	extra pair of (long) socks
water bottle, plastic plates, etc	whistle, torch, compass
anorak (zip opening)	antiseptic cream
sunhat, sunglasses, suncream	small rucksack
spare bootlaces	plastic groundsheet
jacket or woollen shirt	up-to-date bus timetables
gloves	bathing suit, etc

Weather

The average yearly temperature on both islands is 20°C — perfect for hiking. Three chief winds determine the weather on both islands. The **trade wind** (*el alisio*) comes from the **northeast** with speeds of anything up to 25km/h. Its low, fluffy clouds hover over the north for much of the year, lying at a height of 600-1500m (2000-5000ft). They bring lots of moisture and so keep the islands green. However, the southern sides of the islands are much drier and hotter. The *tiempo del sur* is an **easterly or southeasterly** wind which originates over the Sahara and brings hot weather, usually accompanied by fine dust particles. Between November and March, **northwesterly and southwesterly** winds may blow in with storms. Seldom will this ruin an entire day, *but never venture into the mountains when a strong wind is blowing from the west; it's far too dangerous, as it could bring tremendous rainfall within a short time!*

Dogs — and other nuisances

The few **dogs** you'll encounter are mostly all bark, no bite. But if dogs worry you, you might like to invest in a 'Dog Dazer' — an ultrasonic device which persuades aggressive dogs to back off without harming them. These are available from Sunflower Books: contact them for more information (www.sunflowerbooks.co.uk).

Ticks *are* a nuisance: they're prevalent in spring. Keep arms and legs covered, and the problem is solved. On El Hierro, if you're crossing pastures, give **billy goats** a wide berth, and make sure there's a wall/fence between you and the **bulls**! During the hunting season (August to December), **hunters** blasting away may frighten you. Exercise your lungs if you think they're too close. Neither island has any snakes. Although rarely encountered, black widow **spiders** exist on both islands, and also red or black **centipedes**, which also have a dangerous sting.

Country code for walkers and motorists

The experienced rambler is used to following a 'country code', but the tourist out for a lark may unwittingly cause damage, harm animals, and even endanger his own life. Do heed this advice:

- **Do not light fires.** Stub out cigarettes with care.
- **Do not frighten animals.** The goats and sheep you may encounter on your walks are not tame. By making loud noises or trying to touch or photograph them, you may cause them to run in fear and be hurt.

- **Take all your litter away with you.**
- **Walk quietly** through all farms, hamlets and villages, *leaving all gates as you found them.*
- **Protect all wild and cultivated plants.** Don't try to pick wild flowers or uproot saplings. Obviously fruit and crops are someone's private property and should not be touched. *Never walk over cultivated land.*
- **Walkers: do not take risks!** Do not attempt walks beyond your capacity and **never walk alone.** *Always* tell a responsible person *exactly* where you are going and what time you plan to return. Remember:
  — **at any time a walk may become unsafe** due to storm damage or the havoc caused by bulldozers. If the route is not as described in this book, and your way ahead is not secure, *turn back;*
  — **strenuous walks** are unsuitable in high summer;
  — **mountain walks** are unsuitable in wet or very windy weather;
  — **do not overestimate your energies**: your speed will be determined by the slowest walker in the group;
  — **four people** comprise the best walking group. If someone is injured, two people can go for help;
  — **transport connections** at the end of the walk may be vital;
  — **proper shoes or boots** are a necessity;
  — **warm clothing** is needed in the mountains, *even in summer;*
  — **extra food and drink** should be taken on long walks;
  — **always take a sunhat** and cover arms and legs as well;
  — **compass, torch, whistle, first-aid kit, mobile** weigh little, but might save your life. **The emergency number on both islands is 112**.

Spanish for walkers

English is not widely spoken on La Palma, and few people on El Hierro speak it at all. Try to learn a few words of Spanish: although the inhabitants are reserved towards foreigners, they *will* respond warmly to spoken Spanish.

Here's an (almost) foolproof way to communicate in Spanish. First, memorise the few short key questions and their possible answers, given below. Then, when you have your 'mini-speech' memorised, always ask the many questions you can concoct from it **in such a way that you get a 'sí' (yes) or 'no' answer.** Never ask an open-ended question such as 'Where is the main road?' Instead, ask the question and then *suggest the most likely answer yourself.* For instance: 'Good day, sir. Please — where is the path to Los Tilos? *Is it straight ahead?*' Now, unless you get a '*sí*' response, try: '*Is it to the left?*' If you go through the list of answers to your own question, you will eventually get a '*sí*' response … more reassuring than relying solely on sign language.

Following are the two most likely situations in which you may have to practice your Spanish. The dots (…) show where you will fill in the name of your destination. Ask a native (someone at your hotel, a taxi driver) to help you with the pronunciation of place names.

■ Asking the way

The key questions

English	*Spanish*	*pronounced as*
Good day, sir (madam, miss)	Buenos días, señor (señora, señorita)	**Boo**-eh-nos **dee**-ahs, sen-**yor** (sen-**yor**-ah, sen-yor-**ee**-tah)
Please —	Por favor —	**Poor** fa-**vor** —
where is	dónde está	**dohn**-day es-**tah**
the road to …?	la carretera a …?	la cah-reh-**teh**-rah ah …?
the footpath to …?	la senda de …?	lah **sen**-dah day …?
the way to …?	el camino a …?	el cah-**mee**-noh ah …?
the bus stop?	la parada?	lah par-**rah**-dah?
Many thanks.	Muchas gracias.	**Moo**-chas **gra**-thee-as.

Possible answers

English	*Spanish*	*pronounced as*
Is it here?	Está aquí?	Es-**tah** ah-**kee**?
straight ahead?	todo recto?	**toh**-doh rec-toh?
behind?	detrás?	day-**tras**?
to the right?	a la derecha?	ah lah day-**ray**-chah?
to the left?	a la izquierda?	ah lah eeth-kee-**er**-dah?
above?	arriba?	ah-**ree**-bah?
below?	abajo?	ah-**bah**-hoh?

■ Asking a taxi driver to take you somewhere and collect you later in the day

English	*Spanish*	*pronounced as*
Please	Por favor	**Poor** fah-**vor**
take us to …	llévanos a …	l-**yay**-vah-nos ah …
and return	y volver	ee vol-**vair**
for us at … (place)	para nosotros a …	**pah**-rah nos-**oh**-tros ah …
at … (time)	a las …	ah lahs …

(Instead of memorising hours of the day, simply point out the time when you wish to return on your watch, and get his agreement.)

Organisation of the walks

The 16 main walks on La Palma are well dispersed across the island, with several being located near the centre. The four walks on El Hierro are located in the centre and north of the island.

I hope that the book is set out so that you can plan your walks easily … depending on how far you want to go, your abilities and equipment, and what time you are willing to get up in the morning! You might begin by considering the fold-out touring maps inside the back cover. Here you can see at a glance the overall terrain, the road network, and the general orientation of the walking maps in the text.

Quickly flipping through the book, you'll find that there is at least one photograph for every walk. Having selected one or two potential excursions from the map and photographs, look over the planning information at the beginning of each walk description. Here you'll find distance/walking time, grade, equipment, and how to get there by public transport (timetables begin on page 131). If the walk appears to be beyond your fitness or ability, see if a short or alternative version is given, which *does* appeal to you — or look at the map to see if a dashed purple line indicates a waymarked route (see page 36) that you could take as a short-cut back to your car. On hot days, the picnic strolls described on pages 7-10 may be as strenuous an adventure as you'd like to tackle.

When you are on your walk, you will find that the text begins with an introduction to the overall landscape and then turns to a detailed description of the route itself.

Times are given for reaching certain points in the walk. *Important: do* compare your own times with those in the book on one or two short walks, before you set off on a long hike. Remember that I've included only *minimal stops* at viewpoints; allow ample extra time for photography, picnicking, or swimming. Don't forget to take **transport** connections into account!

The large-scale **maps** (all 1:50,000; see page 36) have been set out facing the walking notes if the route is isolated, but where several routes converge, they are often presented on facing pages, to help with overall orientation. Below is a key to the symbols on the maps:

expressway	↦ spring, tank, etc	■ specific building
asphalt road	*P* picnic suggestion (see pages 7-10)	† shrine or cross
major track		⸸ ⟼ church.cemetery
other track	🖼 best views	🏟 stadium
path, steps	🚐 bus stop	⁝ danger! vertigo!
3→ main walk	🚗 car parking	⊔ map continuation
3→ alternative walk	*approximate* route of	*i* visitor centre
watercourse, pipe	PR LP 9 waymarked trail not described in the text	☀ ⌒ mill.cave
—400— altitude (m)	⊓ picnic site with tables	⋀ rock formation
		⩗ blow hole

Walk 1: FROM THE MIRADOR LA TOSCA TO GALLEGOS

Distance/time: 6km/3.7mi; 2h30min

Grade: moderate-strenuous, with total ascents of about 500m/1650ft. You must be sure-footed and have a head for heights. Not recommended in wet weather. *Red and white GR waymarking*

Equipment: walking boots, sunhat, sunglasses, suncream, raingear, long trousers, cardigan, anorak, picnic, water

How to get there: 🚌 from Santa Cruz (Línea 2) to the Barlovento terminus, then ongoing bus (same line) to the Mirador La Tosca; journey time about 1h20min — or walk from Barlovento to the start of the walk (about 15min). Or 🚗: in the parking space next to the *mirador*.
To return: 🚌 from the Gallegos turn-off to Santa Cruz (Línea 2, via Barlovento) or the same bus line back to your car.

This is a roller-coaster walk. Crossing the isolated hills of the northeast, you dip into and out of *barrancos* all the way. But first, enjoy the stupendous view over the rugged north coast from the Mirador La Tosca (**P**1). It's a windswept landscape, where hamlets straggle down the dividing ridges; your hike will take you to Gallegos, the largest of these isolated outposts.

Start out at the **Mirador La Tosca**: walk back towards Barlovento along the main road (LP1). Take the first left turn (**7min**), along a concrete lane signposted 'GR130 — CAMINO REAL DE LA COSTA. GALLEGOS, SANTO DOMINGO'. Three minutes downhill, turn left on a path (signposted 'CAMINO REAL DE GALLEGOS'), descending into the *barranco*. You cross the floor of the *barranco*, passing fallow plots concealed amidst the heather. Soon you round a bend, to enjoy a magnificent view to the distant sea-cliffs on the north coast (**15min**). A path with steps joins you from the left.

Coming onto a driveway in **La Tosca**, pass a house and bear left on the village lane. Ignore minor turn-offs. Meet another lane on a bend (SIGNPOST), and follow it to the right downhill. Two minutes later, the lane swings sharply right: go straight ahead on a concrete path (SIGNPOST), which soon reveals itself as the remains of the old cobbled *camino real*. If the *cumbre* is free of cloud, the white-domed observatory is visible.

Cross the floor of the **Barranco de Topaciegas**, choked with vegetation. After a steep climb up the far side, ignore a path to the left. Keep straight on until you meet a concrete lane (**40min**; SIGNPOST) and follow it uphill to the left. Leave the lane after 30m/yds, turning right on a signposted path. From here you have a good view of the *cumbre* with its seaward-tumbling ridges. Orchards and pockets of cultivation lie scattered across the landscape. Dropping down into another, deeper *barranco* (**Barranco de la Vica**), your way is flanked by sticky *Cistus*. On reaching the other side of the *barranco*, the way is slightly vertiginous for a short stretch. Pass below an old goats' pen lying under a rock overhang.

Leaving the *barranco*, you come onto a road in **La Palmita (1h)**. Ascend the road, cross over another small road, and pick up the signposted continuation of your *camino* some metres uphill. It drops you down into another *barranco*, this one full of bramble bushes. On reaching a track, follow it to the right uphill. A minute later, at an intersection, keep straight on around the hillside. At the fork that follows, go right, downhill (SIGNPOST). Ignore minor tracks striking off left. Gallegos comes into view, looking deceptively close, but it's still two *barrancos* away.

Two minutes below the junction, the track veers right; take the path on the left (SIGNPOST), into the penultimate *barranco*, the **Barranco de Gallegos**. It's the most impressive ... and the most tiring! Winding down its vertical walls, you pass through a gate (please leave it as

Over-looking the north of the island, with the village of La Tosca in the foreground (Picnic 1)

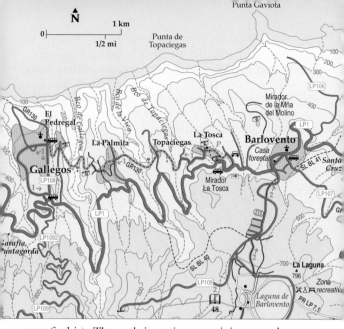

you find it). The path is at times vertiginous and, nearer the bottom, the way might be overgrown. Cross the STREAM BED on boulders (**1h40min**). The climb out of this *barranco* is quite steep. Once out of the *barranco*, beyond another gate, you cross over a road which heads along the crest of the ridge (SIGNPOST). From here you have an excellent view of Gallegos, stepped down a declining rocky ridge. Now the path descends into the final ravine. Once in the bed of this *barranco*, pass some old cave dwellings and turn towards the sea to pick up your ongoing path out of the ravine.

Entering **Gallegos** (**2h**), you reach the main lane at a junction. You could pick up the bus here for the return to your car or to Santa Cruz. Or you could visit the local bar, just 40m/yds downhill. Having quenched your thirst, and wanting to see more of this cute little village, you have two options: Go straight up the road from the bar for 20 minutes, to the main road. The BUS STOP is just opposite the village exit (**2h20min**). Or, for a slightly longer route, turn right at the junction 40m up from the bar. Keep straight on through the simple PLAZA DE LA FUENTE. Picture-postcard dwellings with colourful gardens lie hidden in the midst of vegetable plots, vineyards, orchards and banana groves. Completing the village circuit, climb straight up the hillside for about 25 minutes, back to the main village lane. The main road and the BUS STOP are a minute further uphill (**2h30min**).

Walk 2: LOS SAUCES • MIRADOR DE LAS BARANDAS • BARLOVENTO

Distance: 12km/7.5mi; 4h10min

Grade: strenuous, with an overall ascent of 900m/3000ft. The path out of the Barranco de Herradura is steep, narrow and vertiginous. You must be sure-footed and have a head for heights. Don't attempt in wet weather. *Yellow and white PR waymarking along most of the walk*

Equipment: walking boots, sunhat, sunglasses, suncream, warm cardigan, raingear, picnic, plenty of water. A walking stick would be a great help on the narrow path!

How to get there: 🚌 from Santa Cruz to Los Sauces (Línea 2); journey time 50min. Or 🚗: park in Los Sauces.
To return: 🚌 from Barlovento to Santa Cruz (Línea 2); journey time about 1h20min. Or the same line to Los Sauces, to collect your car.

The north boasts the most impressive ravines on the island, like the unmissable Barranco de Herradura. A forestry track leads you into this *barranco*, and a footpath not much wider than a pair of boots takes you back out of it. On the way in, you'll see magnificent colonies of La Palma's endemic blue *Echium* (viper's bugloss), a rival for Tenerife's *taginaste rojo* both in splendour and in height. *Woodwardia radicans,* a prehistoric fern with 2-3 metre-long stems, flourishes on the damp *barranco* walls.

Begin the walk at the BUS STOP in **Los Sauces**. Cross the street and walk 10m/yds to the left. Then go uphill (at the right of a park), past the Ayuntamiento (town hall) and the pharmacy. Keep straight uphill, climbing steeply. This village has an authentic farmyard feel about it. Some of the old homes will take you by surprise with their unusually bright colours, while the gardens display a mixture of flowers, fruit trees and vegetables.

A renovated AQUEDUCT on the left will catch your eye (**10min**). Just past the aqueduct, turn right (signpost: PICO DE LA CRUZ, MIRADOR TOPO DE LAS BARANDAS, PR LP7). Not far uphill, the road forks. Both forks rejoin, but take the left fork — it's quicker. Once past the CAMPO DE FUTBOL, the climb steepens, as you rise through patchy cultivation. Soon after the forks have rejoined and the way has reverted to track, you reach the rim of **Barranco del Agua** (**30min**), with an excellent view towards the *cumbre*.

From this lookout point, leave the track and climb a cobbled path to the left (SIGNPOST). Several minutes up, on rejoining the track (SIGNPOST), follow it to the left uphill. The steadily ascending track winds through scrub, a mixture of laurels, heather, ferns, *codeso (Adenocarpus),* and scatterings of old chestnut trees, while the Barranco de Herradura drops away to the right.

Ignore all turn-offs until you reach the turn-off left to the **Mirador de las Barandas** (**1h10min**). From the *mirador* you enjoy the splendid view shown opposite, looking straight down into the Barranco del Agua and across the heavily-wooded ridges that carve up the landscape.

Return the 120m/yds to the main track, to continue the walk. Ignore a first track off right but, 10 minutes from the *mirador,* fork right on a clear track (signpost: LAGUNA DE BARLOVENTO, PR LP7.1). Every now and then you'll see enormous viper's bugloss along the route. In summer their 2-3m/6-9ft-high stalks will be embellished with blue flowers. The native white-tailed and Bolle's laurel pigeons abound up here too. Ignore a faint track to the left after approximately 20 minutes (SIGNPOST). The prehistoric fern colonies *(Woodwardia Radicans)* along this part of the walk are the largest on the whole island.

Entering the **Barranco de Herradura**, the way becomes dark and shady. A rockfall has caused the track to narrow down to a path. As you approach the valley floor, notice the caves cut into the bank on the left, just before the track turns sharply to the right. A couple of minutes further along, go into the trees on a waymarked path. In just one minute you reach the **Galería Meleno** (**2h10min**), securely locked behind a metal gate. There's an ABANDONED BUILDING on the left side of the ravine; some endemic geraniums grow beside the track.

The continuing path begins at the right of the abandoned building and is steep and vertiginous at the outset. The slopes are sheer, but wooded, thus lessening the exposure … at least psychologically. ***Important:*** *remember that the leaves covering the path are very slippery.* A good 10 minutes up, you round a bend and enter another shady mossy *barranco* with vertical walls; not only is this ravine so dark that it's difficult to appreciate its beauty, but your eyes *should* be glued to the path the whole time!

Close on 30 minutes up from the *barranco* floor, you rise to a CREST (**2h40min**; PR LP7.1 signpost). The path takes you to a track, soon flanked by garden plots. The Laguna de Barlovento (a large reservoir) appears through the trees, with a *zona recreativa* to its right. The surrounding hills are being cleared of trees and scrub to create gardens and orchards. Minutes out of the *barranco,* when you come to a T-junction, turn left (where a SIGNPOST points in the *opposite* direction). The *laguna* reappears not far ahead; later in the walk you will circle to the left of it.

Now ignore all side paths and tracks for the next 10 minutes, until you come to a major junction (SIGNPOSTS): turn right here. Now keep to the main track, ignoring all side tracks. Twenty minutes from the major junction, weave your way past a few buildings (visitors' centres and museums for a 'rural interpretation park' — *still* in the making, after about 14 years!). When you reach a junction with a large orange building on the corner below, turn right and after a minute join the road to the **Laguna de Barlovento** *zona recreativa* (**3h35min**). Turn left; then,

The Barranco del Agua from the Mirador de las Barandas

some 50m/yds along, leave the road: turn right on a track, heading into a cultivated basin. Ignore the fork to the right at the outset. Follow the same path/track, ignoring all turn-offs, until you reach the main road. Turn right for 100m/yds, then go left into a small industrial area. When you reach the main road again, cross it and follow the track opposite, again ignoring side paths. Cross the road again and continue on a path, straight past cultivated fields and a housing estate on the left. Reaching the main Barlovento/Gallegos road, follow it to the left, then take the second right turn, just before a *casa forestal* (forestry house). This brings you to the centre of **Barlovento** (**4h10min**). The BUS STOP is 100m/yds below the CENTRO DE SALUD.

Walk 3: LAS LOMADAS • BARRANCO DEL AGUA • LOS TILOS • LOS SAUCES

See map opposite; see also photograph page 47

Distance/time: 10km/6.2mi; 3h35min

Grade: strenuous. There's a lot of scrambling over rocks and boulders in the bed of the *barranco,* and a climb of 350m/1100ft to the *mirador.* You must be sure-footed and have a head for heights. Don't attempt just after rain or in very windy weather: the paths are dangerous if wet, and there is the possibility of rockfall in the *barranco. Yellow and white PR waymarking beyond Los Tilos*

Equipment: hiking boots, sunhat, sunglasses, suncream, anorak, rain-gear, picnic, water, *torch*

How to get there and return: 🚌 or 🚗 from Santa Cruz to Las Lomadas (🚌 Línea 2); alight/park just before the bridge over the Barranco del Agua; journey time 45min. *Hint: You will not see the bridge from the bus in time to alight, so make it clear to the driver that you are walking to Los Tilos.* Return on the same bus from Los Sauces, or walk back to your car (add 15min). 🚗 Or motorists could park at Los Tilos and at the end of the walk take a taxi from the square in Los Sauces back to their car.

Short walks

1 **Los Tilos — Mirador de las Barandas — Los Tilos** (2km/1.25mi; 1h). Grade (ascent) and equipment as main walk. 🚗 car or taxi to/from Los Tilos (car park). Climb the steep path ascending the hillside from the car park (behind the Interpretation Centre, the 2h-point in the main walk). Take care when returning: the descent is slippery!

2 **Los Tilos — Barranco del Agua — Los Tilos** (1km/0.6mi; 30min return). Easy, but you need to be agile — there's lots of scrambling over and around rocks (wear stout shoes with a good grip). Don't attempt in wet or windy weather. 🚗 as Short walk 1. From the car park walk down the asphalt road a short way, to locate a watercourse with adjacent path — on your right, 100m/yds before the bridge. Pick up the main walk at the 1h-point and follow it to the first rock face.

There's no *barranco* like this one in the whole archipe-lago. Its virtually perpendicular walls are smothered in vegetation, and from its boulder-strewn floor you look up at the sky through cascading ferns and trees. In summer, only one thing is missing from the Barranco del Agua … water. Narrow *canales* divert this precious commodity higher up the valley, transporting it to nearby villages and farms, and to a power plant that generates 10 per cent of the island's electricity.

The walk begins in **Las Lomadas**, at the BUS STOP just south of the BRIDGE OVER THE BARRANCO DEL AGUA. Follow the road into the *barranco,* then take the left turn (**15min**) and ascend the road towards Los Tilos. In about **1h** you cross the Barranco del Agua for the third time: 100m/yds further on, on a bend in the road, look below the road on the left for a watercourse with an adjacent path. *(Short Walk 2 joins here and turns right on the watercourse.)* Follow this path for a minute, until you reach a TANK, then take steps down into the bed of the *barranco*. (Or take the alternative route and go through the short TUNNEL in the right-hand side of the *barranco* wall — if you've brought your torch.) Depending on the time of the year when you're walking and how much water is in the *barranco*, you should be able to venture from 10 minutes to half an hour upstream — scrambling over tree trunks, rocks and, eventually, boulders, and encountering steep drops. Sometimes a large WATERFALL about 200m past the tunnel will block your way — unless you want to get soaking wet! It's not always there, but in winter it acts as an overflow for some of the excess water in the *canals* above. *Only go as far as you feel comfortable and safe.* If you get far enough, you'll reach the end of the walkable part of the *barranco* — a sheer cliff face, where you will have to turn back.

Back on the road, turn left to the car park and restaurant at **Los Tilos** and, above these, the INTERPRETATION CENTRE ('Biosphere Reserve'; **2h**). There's a large picnic area below the centre but, for a more peaceful spot, try the setting shown below (Picnic 3): locate the watercourse two minutes' walk below the centre and follow it to the left for a few minutes. The path is vertiginous, but a handrail *(don't lean on it)* provides psychological support.

The next part of the walk is the tiring climb to the Mirador de las Barandas. Take the yellow/white way-marked path behind the centre (large board: CAMINO AL MIRADOR DE LAS BARANDAS). There are no turn-offs. Handrails along the vertiginous stretches help allay any fears, but *don't lean on them!* Thirty-five minutes up, and blue in the face, you reach the **Mirador de las Barandas** (**2h35min**; photograph page 47), with a shelter, tables and benches, and a water tap. From here you look straight up the ravine as it twists and winds its way into the laurel woods of the central massif. Los Tilos lies below, in the narrow V of the *barranco*.

To make for Los Sauces, follow the track from the *mirador* to the main track and descend right on the PR LP7, ignoring all turn-offs. Through the trees and scrub you catch glimpses of the Barranco de Herradura (Walk 2), which soon drops away to your left. Some 30 minutes from the *mirador,* turn right on a cobbled path (SIGNPOST), just above an S-bend. After this short-cut you rejoin the main track on the very edge of the Barranco del Agua (**3h10min**) — with a bird's-eye view of the tremendous *barranco* of Los Tilos.

Two minutes later the way becomes concreted and divides. Take the right fork, to begin the steep descent to Los Sauces. This pretty farming settlement is spread across a shoulder in the hillside, completely enveloped by banana plantations. Passing the *campo de fútbol*, you rejoin the left fork and continue downhill. A road joins from the right; a couple of minutes later, bear right at a fork. Multicoloured houses briefly flank the street leading into the centre of **Los Sauces** (**3h35min**). The BUS STOP is to the left of the main square, opposite the CHURCH.

Left: watercourse at Los Tilos (Picnic 3); right: in the Barranco del Agua the walls, dripping with vegetation, tower overhead and block out the sun.

Walk 4: CASA DEL MONTE • NACIENTES DE MARCOS • NACIENTES DE CORDERO • LOS TILOS

See also cover photograph   **Distance/time:** 12km/7.5mi; 4h15min

Grade: very strenuous, with an ascent of about 150m/500ft and drawn-out descent of some 900m/3000ft. You must be sure-footed and have a head for heights: for about 1h20min the walk follows a *canal* cut into the sheer *barranco* wall. Only attempt this walk during a spell of fine, stable weather, and turn back *immediately* if the weather deteriorates. Do *not* attempt the walk just after bad weather, as there is a danger of rockfall and landslides. There are 13 tunnels on this walk, some narrow: not recommended for those who suffer from claustrophobia! *Yellow and white PR waymarks on most of the route, as well as white/green poles from the Casa del Monte up to the springs of Cordero.*

Equipment: walking boots, raingear, jacket, trousers, picnic, water, *plus torch, large plastic bag, and an extra pair of socks* (one of the tunnels is as wet as a power shower: cover both yourself and your rucksack!).

How to get there: 🚗 to Los Tilos: park at the foot of the first track on the left, 2km up the Los Tilos road (500m short of the visitors' centre). Or 🚌 from Santa Cruz to/from Las Lomadas (Línea 2); alight just before the bridge over the Barranco del Agua; journey time 45min. (Allow an extra 55min *each way* from the bus stop by the bridge to the track where the walk begins and back down to the main road.) From Los Tilos 4x4 taxi to the Casa del Monte to start the walk — an exhilarating drive of some 50min on a dirt track. Taxis are available every day: either call and make an appointment with Toño (629-213435), Luis (616-

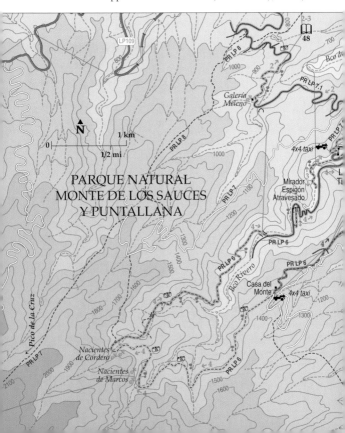

418847) or Pepe (649-945481) — they all speak a bit of English — or just show up at Los Tilos on the day: a taxi will be on duty. In general the drivers arrive at Los Tilos between 09.00-09.30 and try to fill their taxis, so there may be a short wait. Cost € 15 per person at press date.

Short walk: Los Tilos — Mirador Espigón Atravesado — Los Tilos (5km/3mi; 1h30min). Moderate, with an ascent of 250m/820ft. Access and equipment as above (excluding tunnel equipment), but stout shoes will suffice. Follow the track signposted 'MONTE EL CANAL Y LOS TILOS' that leads into the forest from the lower parking area (the main walk in reverse). After 50min you come to the junction at the 3h35min-point in the main walk. Just below it, take the path to the left, to a precarious and vertiginous (but brilliant!) viewpoint over the ravine (3-5min). Return the same way.

Alternative walk: Casa del Monte — Nacientes de Cordero — Casa del Monte — Las Lomadas (18km/11mi; 6h). This gives you the thrill of the *canal* stretch and the tunnels (twice!), but avoids the bouldery sections in the Barranco Rivero. The final stretch to Las Lomadas is via a beautiful tunnel-like path (to stay with the theme of the day) through the laurel forest. Grade and access as main walk (🚌 to Las Lomadas and walk up to Los Tilos at the start of the day, when you are fresh (3km, with a height gain of 200m/650ft) — or try to hitch a ride up!) Return by bus from Las Lomadas. Pick up the 4x4 taxi at Los Tilos and follow the main walk to the 1h30min-point, then see notes on page 57. Travelling by car, it's best to drive to Los Tilos, make taxi arrangements, then drive back to Las Lomadas to park and hop on the taxi to Casa del Monte.

This walk can be summed up in three words: exhilarating, breathtaking (in more ways than one), and tiring. You start the walk high up in an isolated valley, following an irrigation *canal* with 13 tunnels — a marvel of workmanship. It's my favourite walk on the island, even though cliff-hanging watercourses give me the jitters. Your reward is water splashing down out of the hillsides once you reach the *nacientes* (springs) of Marcos and Cordero. This is followed by a scramble over rocks and boulders through an impressive *barranco,* which is not unlike the one in the Caldera de Taburiente, until you eventually reach a good but long, drawn-out descent path through a 'jungle' of laurel woods.

Begin the walk at the drop-off point near the **Casa del Monte**, at a height of 1330m/4360ft, where a gushing open *canal* meets the track. There are some large boards here, with information about the trail. Follow the *canal* to the left through the laurel forest. You will be walking along this watercourse for about an hour and 20 minutes — sometimes you will need to scramble up onto the edge of it but, in general, the path runs alongside it.

After five minutes the views open up and an immense *barranco* lies at your feet, with drops of several hundred meters. A rickety railing offers some psychological protection, but *don't lean on it!* There are also many steep and narrow sections still without railings, so *please watch where you're walking all the time. To appreciate the magnificent scenery, stop walking, then look!*

Some 10 minutes along the FIRST OF THE 13 TUNNELS presents itself; at the outset it seems straightforward — wide and high — but, just 10m/yds in, this changes drastically into a narrow passage with steps leading down into the dark. The floor is probably covered in puddles, so if you haven't worn waterproof walking boots, it's too late now! The THIRD AND LONGEST TUNNEL (350m/yds) is a narrow affair and quite a squeeze, very romantic … especially when you meet a group of 20 other sweaty hikers halfway through!

Continue winding your way around the steep hillside, taking in the tremendous drops and the game of clouds filling in the canyon from time to time.

After tackling the NINTH TUNNEL (**55min**) you get a grand view of what is still in store for you. To the right, strain to see your ongoing path to the springs of Cordero through a gap in the inaccessible-looking cliff face. Straight ahead is a dark vertical wall pierced with holes, where you'll encounter the (in)famous 12TH TUNNEL, where you'll have your 'power shower'. All the while, the sound of water gets stronger. Put all your cameras and other delicate equipment away and cover yourself up with plastic bags to tackle this 'amusement park tunnel', with water coming out of the walls from all angles and a small river at your feet.

When you emerge in the sunshine at the other end, probably drenched, you reach the first springs en route, the **Nacientes de Marcos (1h 10min)**, where water spouts out of the mountainside in small cascades.

Now haul yourself up the steep path up along the raging stream until you reach a higher *canal*. One more TUNNEL awaits you before you reach the second springs, the **Nacientes de Cordero** (**1h30min**). *(The Alternative walk turns back here; see notes on page 57.)*

Leave the springs and head into the canyon by taking the clear path to the right of the springs. After five minutes you enter the riverbed and cross it. Some enormous boulders may appear to block your way, but waymarking guides you round them. Then follow the path on the left-hand side of the *barranco*, only to cross back to the other side after a few minutes. Stay on

Right: some of the plants you will see on La Palma include (from top to bottom) taginaste, vinagrera, codeso, verode, red-flowering tabaiba and candelabra spurge.

this path for 10 minutes and cross again to the LEFT SIDE OF THE RIVERBED (**1h 50min**). When you regain the barranco bed after a good five minutes, follow it down to the left, scrambling (occasionally on all fours) over rocks, boulders and tree trunks, avoiding small puddles and wet walls dripping with beautiful colonies of prehistoric ferns, the *Woodwardia radicans*. Little light penetrates this dark fissure.

After 20 minutes in the *barranco* bed, you come to a SIGNPOST and a path on the right, which takes you across a WOODEN BRIDGE (**2h25min**). The torture is over, and you are now on a good but drawn-out path that will take you all the way down to Los Tilos. *But don't let your guard down:* in some places the path narrows, with steep drops. Eventually the valley opens up ahead, but then you enter the laurel forest once more and, the further down you go, the more the path is shaded with dense foliage. After an hour down this path you cross the deep **Barranco Rivero** on another WOODEN BRIDGE (**3h25min**), this one more imposing (but *don't* lean on the handrail!). Climb up to the main Los Tilos track and follow it down to the left, again passing enormous colonies of ferns.

Sometimes you'll be walking on the very lip of the canal, *but usually there is an adjacent path.*

Ten minutes later, at a junction of paths and an INFORMATION BOARD (**3h35min**), turn right up a narrow and vertiginous path to the **Mirador Espigón Atravesado**, a brilliant view point overlooking the dense jungle of Los Tilos. *(The short walk comes up to this point from Los Tilos, then returns the same way)*. Then, ignoring all side paths, follow the main track down to the parking area below **Los Tilos** (**4h15min**).

Alternative walk

From the **Nacientes de Cordero** (**1h30min**) make your way back through the tunnels to the point where the taxi dropped you off in the morning near the **Casa del Monte**. Turn right on a path opposite this building (**3h**). Three minutes down, the path narrows and veers sharply left downhill. For the next 30 minutes your route goes straight down this dark, heavily-wooded path, until you reach the MOTORABLE TRACK TO LAS LOMADAS (**3h30min**; SIGNPOST). *Don't* join the motor track here, but continue on the path; 10m/yds further down you rejoin the track (SIGNPOST). Walk 10m/yds to the left and then branch off on the path again (SIGNPOST). When you next meet the track, follow it 50m/yds down to the left to rejoin the path (SIGNPOST). Next you emerge on a minor farm track: go 10m/yds to the right here, to pick up the path again, a deep trench cut into the hillside. A T-junction follows: turn right along the track. After one minute another track joins from the right. One minute later, at a three-way junction, cross a track and descend a COBBLED PATH (**4h05min**; SIGNPOST).

After five minutes the path meets the end of an overgrown track; turn left here. After another five minutes follow a concrete lane descending ahead. Two minutes later turn right along a track and, after 10m/yds, pick up the old path again. For the next five minutes keep straight downhill on this narrow path, beside a WATER PIPE. Meet a track and follow it to the left. Cross another track and after 25m/yds, you can pick up the washed-out path, on the left. When you rejoin the MAIN TRACK at a fork, go left (SIGNPOST). At the junction 30m/yds further on, fork left (signpost, 'LAS LOMADAS'). Pass a WHITE BUILDING and continue downhill on a concrete lane. Los Sauces sits on the slopes opposite. From here, just keep straight downhill, first on the concrete lane and then an asphalt road. Passing through **Las Lomadas**, you reach the LP1. The BUS STOP is just where you join the main road (**5h**).

Walk 5: BARRANCO DE LA GALGA

Distance/time: 4.5km/3mi; 1h35min

Grade: easy, with a gradual ascent of 250m/820ft, all along a wide track. Recommended for everyone. *Yellow and white PR waymarking for much of the way; also green and white auto-guiding trail markings*

Equipment: walking shoes, raingear, cardigan, picnic, water

How to get there and return: 🚌 from Santa Cruz to the north (Línea 2); alight at the second tunnel just after La Galga (bus drivers know the stop); journey time about 30min; same bus to return. Or by 🚗: park just before the second tunnel north of La Galga.

Alternative walk: descending through a chestnut grove on the slippery cobbled path above La Galga

Alternative walk: Barranco de la Galga — Cubo de la Galga — La Galga (6.8km/4.2mi; 1h40min by bus; 6.4km/4mi by car). Grade as main walk. However, the path out of the *barranco* is vertiginous; you must be sure-footed and have a head for heights. Walking boots are recommended. Access as main walk. Follow the main walk to just past the 40min-point, to the recess in the valley wall. Facing the cliffs, take the path straight ahead that passes underneath the watercourse via a little arch. Then, at the junction, turn left (SIGNPOST) and follow this path along the steep *barranco*. Be careful after rainfall, parts of the path may have fallen away. Within 20min, when you reach a concrete track (signpost: PR LP5.1, LA GALGA, SAN BARTOLOME), follow it downhill past a bus turning point, when asphalt comes underfoot. A few minutes later, in a big bend to the right (with a SIGNPOST as above), turn left downhill on a slippery cobbled path beside a pipe. Descending through a chestnut grove, you reach a concrete lane surrounded by fields. Follow the lane down past a line of houses. After 5min, cross straight over a road, onto an embankment. A concrete lane follows. If you came by car, turn left here by a sign, 'PUNTO INFORMACION 1KM' and after 15m/yds turn right on a concrete path (a covered watercourse). After 50m/yds turn right on a narrow, overgrown trail and cross a water pipe. In 10 minutes you reach your outgoing lane. Turn right, back to the information hut and your car. If you came by bus, at the 'PUNTO' sign cross the road again, keeping straight down on a concrete lane which takes you under the road. Then cross the road once again and descend to the main road in La Galga (1h40min; signpost pointing back to 'CUBO DE LA GALGA'. The bus stop is 5m/yds to the left of this junction.

Canary pine

Canary palm

Dragon tree

This walk is ideal for 'first timers'. It's just straight up and straight back without any paths turning off to confuse you, and you get a taste of La Palma's laurel forest without having to venture too far.

Begin at the BUS STOP AT THE TUNNEL: take the narrow road leading up the **Barranco de la Galga**, at the left of the INFORMATION HUT. Ignore the track descending to the left. From the outset you can see that this is a deep ravine, with walls matted in vegetation. Billowing bushes of blackberry border the route. You pass a small grove of chestnut trees almost lost in this turmoil of vegetation. The sound of water trickling down the walls provides company for most of the way.

After **15min** the tarmac ends; the track passes below an AQUEDUCT (**25min**) and soon the floor of the *barranco* fills with laurel trees. Fifteen minutes later both the

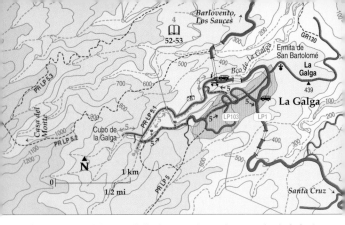

barranco and the track fork (**40min**). First try the left fork. This track ends almost immediately, but a path leads up to a small waterfall (in winter) in a few minutes. *Geranium canariense* abounds along the floor of the *barranco*. On the left lies a beautiful recess in the valley wall, shaded by tall thin trees, where you will see a *canal* and a large water pipe. *(Those doing the Alternative walk turn left just past the* canal, *but first have a look into the right fork of the* barranco.*)*

Return to the fork and turn left on a track. Ignore a turning left with a turnstile. The track ends in a clearing where a small trail with dense vegetation leads you further into a rock cauldron, the **Cubo de la Galga** (**55min**). Quarrying once took place here, but now the massive escarpment has reverted to nature. After heavy rain a pretty waterfall flows down the hanging valley opposite.

Allow yourself about 40min to return to the BUS STOP ON THE MAIN ROAD (**1h35min**). If you've plenty of time to spare before the bus, there's a bar-restaurant in La Galga, 20 minutes uphill to the right, and another bus stop just beyond it (where a lane ascends to the right).

Laurel forest in the Barranco de la Galga

Walk 6: LP4 (PICO DE LA NIEVE TURN-OFF) • PICO DE LA NIEVE • PUNTA DE LOS ROQUES • ERMITA DE LA VIRGEN DEL PINO • NATIONAL PARK VISITOR CENTRE

Distance/time: 16km/10mi; 5h45min

Grade: moderate but long, with an initial ascent of 300m/1000ft and a descent of 1400m/4600ft. Accessible to all sturdy hill walkers who are sure-footed and have a head for heights, but only suitable in fine weather. Avoid on very windy days. At times the path may be overgrown with *codeso*. **Important:** *Weather conditions can change rapidly; be prepared! If cloud descends,* **utmost care** *is needed, as the walk edges the rim of the crater for much of the way. Both yellow/white (PR) and red/white (GR) waymarking*

Equipment: walking boots, sunhat (and something to tie it on with!), sunglasses, suncream, long-sleeved shirt, long trousers, warm cardigan, warm jacket, gloves, raingear, picnic, plenty of water

How to get there: ⇌ taxi to the Pico de la Nieve turn-off on the LP4; journey time 35min from Santa Cruz
To return: ⇌ from the National Park Visitor Centre (Línea 1) — to Santa Cruz (journey time 40min) or Los Llanos (journey time 20min)

Short walk: LP4 (Pico de la Nieve turn-off) to Pico de la Nieve and return (4.75km/3mi; 2h). Moderate ascent of 300m/1000ft. Equipment and access as main walk or ⇌ (*4x4 only!*) to a parking area at the end of the Pico de la Nieve track (saves 100m/330ft; 20min of climbing). Follow the main walk to the 1h15min-point, then turn left. Ten minutes later rejoin your outgoing path and turn right downhill, back to your car.

Alternative walks

1   Cruce del Refugio — Ermita de la Virgen del Pino — Reventón Pass — Refugio El Pilar — National Park Visitor Centre (16.5km/10mi; 5h20min). Strenuous, with an ascent of 580m/1900ft. Equipment as main walk. Access by ⇌ to Cruce del Refugio (Línea 1); journey time from Santa Cruz 40min. From the junction where you leave the bus walk north along the main road for 50m/yds, then turn left on a country road. Use the map to walk to the Ermita de la Virgen del Pino (40min) and then ascend to the Reventón Pass (1h55min). Turn right at the pass and, referring to the map on pages 68-69, follow the track to the Refugio El Pilar (3h35min). To end the walk, pick up Walk 7 at the 2h20min-point.

2   Ermita de la Virgen del Pino — Refugio de la Punta de los Roques — Ermita de la Virgen del Pino (17km/10.5mi; 6h10min). Very strenuous, with an ascent of 1250m/4100ft. Only suitable in fine weather. Equipment as main walk. Access by ⇌: park at the *ermita*, north of the National Park Visitor Centre. Or ⇌ to/from the National Park Visitor Centre (Línea 1; journey time from Santa Cruz 40min; add 30min *each way* to the walking times above). Referring to the map on page 63, follow this section of the main walk in reverse — from either the *ermita* or the visitor centre; return the same way.

I consider this one of the top walks in the Canaries. Circling the Caldera de Taburiente, often on its very rim, spectacular views unfold. On the descent the outlook sweeps across the plain of Los Llanos, over the volcanoes of El Pilar, and along the *cumbre*. If you're reasonably fit, this is *one walk you've got to do!* And the good news is that a taxi or hired car will do most of the climbing for you.

61

Start out at the PICO DE LA NIEVE TURN-OFF. Walk up the LP4 for 10m/yds, then take the hillside path above the road (signpost: PICO LA NIEVE, PR LP3). After a couple of minutes, the path swings back left, then climbs a gentle slope and widens out. Cairns mark the way through a typical Canary pine forest — spacious and with a floor clear of scrub. The path takes you to a CAR PARK (*where the Short walk can begin and end;* **20min**) and continues uphill for another 15 minutes; here you turn right on the path to the summit (SIGNPOST). Your view stretches across the forested shoulders of the *cumbre* — on clear days to Tenerife and La Gomera in the distance. Santa Cruz sits far below.

Approaching the edge of the crater, turn right uphill on the GR131 (signpost: ROQUE DE LOS MUCHACHOS). (Ignore signposting for the Refugio del Pilar to the left.) At the next fork, keep left (the right-hand fork leads to Roque de los Muchachos). From the SUMMIT OF **Pico de la Nieve** (**1h**) a breathtaking view opens before you, of a deep cauldron lined by sheer ridges. The white buildings peeping over the crater walls on the right belong to the observatory shown on page 18.

Return to the Roque de los Muchachos junction and turn right; turn right again at the next fork (signpost: REFUGIO DEL PILAR). Along this stretch, several short paths branch off right to viewpoints on the edge of the *caldera*. A path joins from the left (**1h15min**); follow it to the right. (*But for the Short walk, turn left.*) After a few minutes, you cross the pass of **Degollada del Barranco de la Madera**. Here you'll notice some very colourful rocky outcrops rising out of the crater wall. A few minutes later you encounter a signposted turn-off left to some petroglyphs ('PETROGLIFO TAGOROR PICO DE LA SABINA') and, above and to the right, a sign indicating some old shepherds' huts and corrals. Some 200m further on the petroglyph detour path rejoins, then you pass a bald gravel mound in hues of mauve, pink, smoky blue, and rusty brown.

The next section of the hike is the most striking. A zig-zag descent leads you down and across another pass—the **Degollada del Río** (**2h05min**). The ridge here is narrow and slides away on either side of the path. The huge valley to the left is the Barranco de la Hortelana, while to the right the crater just opens into a bottomless abyss. A steep climb follows, up the side of a precipitous jagged crag. Back on the inside of the crater, you pass by the eye-catching weather-beaten *cedro* shown above. Ahead is a magnificent viewpoint. In the depths of this cataclysm of

Right: a noticeable weather-beaten cedro *is passed just before the refuge; far right: striding along the* cumbre *on the descent to Reventón Pass. Below left: leaving the Cruce del Refugio, you soon look across a basin of fields criss-crossed by stone walls (Alternative walk 1). Below right: view south from the Refugio de la Punta de los Roques over the El Paso basin to the Cumbre Vieja*

rock, you can see the floor of the Barranco de Taburiente and a corner of the Playa de Taburiente (Walk 11). Then you round a bend and arrive at the **Refugio de la Punta de los Roques (2h35min)**. Although there is no heating, and fires are prohibited, the shelter may be welcome nonetheless. There are wooden bunks where you can lay out a sleeping bag, and water is available in bottles. The slope falling from the refuge overlooks the extensive open valleys of El Paso and Los Llanos. The big hump of a mountain bordering the *caldera* on the south side is Bejenado (Walk 10), with Cumbre Vieja (Walk 9) in the background.

Continuing, pick up the path below the refuge. The route descends the *cumbre*, never straying far from the crest. Ignore a path to the left 10 minutes past **Pico Corralejo** (PR LP2) and another five minutes past the sign for **Pico Ovejas** (PR LP2.1). The western side of the *cumbre* opens up, affording another fine view over Santa Cruz. The path finally drops down onto the **Pista Cumbre**

Nueva. Continue ahead on this wide forestry track. Some 20 minutes later you arrive at **Reventón Pass (4h25min)**, where there is a WATER TAP. Fork right downhill here on the PR LP1 (signpost: ERMITA DE LA VIRGEN DEL PINO).

A beautiful old cobbled path leads you down the steep slope, below trees festooned with lichen and beside moss-covered rocks. A basin of small fields lies below. Five minutes down, a path joins from the right. Some 30 minutes down, you descend a splendid 'avenue' of regal Canary pines, some reputedly 400 to 500 years old. A signposted path from La Cumbrecita joins from the right here. Five minutes later you join a faint track leading to the **Ermita de la Virgen del Pino** (5h15min; Picnic 6).

The National Park Visitor Centre is just under half an hour away: follow the road from the chapel and, after 15 minutes, at a junction, turn left. On reaching the LP3, turn left again to the **Visitor Centre (5h45min)**. The Santa Cruz bus stops opposite.

Walk 7: LOMO DE LOS MESTRES • LA PARED VIEJA • REFUGIO EL PILAR • NATIONAL PARK VISITOR CENTRE

Distance/time: 15km/9.3mi; 4h10min

Grade: moderate; gradual ascent of 450m/1500ft. Not recommended in wet weather. *Yellow and white PR waymarking for most of the way. Note: new paths and tracks are established in this area every few months, to reach wood-cutting areas and newly-established fields. Some new paths and tracks may be missing from the text and the maps, but the walk is easily followed if you watch for the signposts and waymarks. Around the Pared Vieja picnic area, as well as if you are doing the Alternative walk, do not follow the small white/green signposts, but the white/yellow waymarking.*

Equipment: walking shoes, sunhat, sunglasses, suncream, raingear, warm cardigan, anorak, picnic, water

How to get there: 🚌 Los Llanos bus *from Santa Cruz* (Línea 1). ***Important notes:*** There are two tunnels on the LP3 below Cumbre Nueva, and traffic is one-way: from Santa Cruz to Los Llanos through the old tunnel and from Los Llanos to Santa Cruz through the newer, lower tunnel. The walk is only accessible from the *older tunnel.* If you are taking a bus from Los Llanos, you must go into Santa Cruz and then switch to a bus travelling *back* to Los Llanos. (If you are travelling by taxi from Los Llanos, your driver will have to go through the new tunnel first, then head back up the *cumbre* towards the old tunnel.) By bus or taxi, ask to be dropped off just before the 'túnel viejo', an *unofficial bus stop* not far below the old tunnel; journey time 35min from Santa Cruz. ***Important note:*** despite the fact that there is a large lay-by before the tunnel and this walk is in all the guides, some drivers *refuse to stop.* Before you board, ask for '**la entrada del túnel viejo de la cumbre, la pista que va a la Pared Vieja**'; if necessary, show the driver this text or the map. Do not board unless you have the driver's agreement, because you cannot alight past the tunnel and walk back (walking and cycling through the tunnel is forbidden). If the driver refuses, you will have to take a taxi.

To return: 🚌 same bus from the National Park Visitor Centre; journey time 40min to Santa Cruz

Short walk: Refugio El Pilar — National Park Visitor Centre (6.5km/4mi; 2h). Easy, with a descent of 600m/1950ft. Equipment as main walk. Access by 🚕 taxi or with friends to the Refugio El Pilar. Follow the main walk from just after the 2h20min-point to the end and return as in the main walk.

Other short walks from the Refugio El Pilar: Users have written about two walks they enjoyed; these paths are shown on the map, but *not* highlighted. All start by continuing south from the *refugio* on the signposted GR131. 1) After 45min turn off right on signposted SL EP104 and follow this down to a forestry road, then turn right back to El Pilar. 2) After 1h stay left on the track (ignoring the path to the right followed in Walk 9); rise steeply in zigzags up a firebreak and then round Montaña de la Barquita and Pico Birigoyo, before descending to the *refugio*. And don't miss the Short circular walk: Birigoyo — or Ruta de los Volcanes 'lite' on page 78, which also starts at El Pilar.

Alternative walk: Lomo de los Mestres — La Pared Vieja — Cumbre Nueva — Mazo (16.5km/10.3mi; 4h40min). Moderate, with an ascent of 450m/1500ft and a descent of 950m/3100ft, much of it down an old cobbled path (slippery in wet weather). Equipment and access as main walk. Return by bus to Santa Cruz (Línea 3) or pick up a taxi when you reach Mazo. I highly recommend this hike: the stretch from the Pista

Cumbre Nueva to Mazo follows one of the finest old *caminos* (cobbled trails) on the island. It's called **El Camino de la Faya** (The Heath Tree Trail). Follow the main walk up to the 2h20min-point, where it briefly joins the Pista Cumbre Nueva. From here follow the El Pilar/San Isidro road uphill to the left. After 400m/yds, note a forestry track to the right called PF111 Llano de la Mosca. Some 50m/yds beyond this track, turn left between two low stone walls (yellow and white waymarking). Soon a track joins from the right and the path widens out. A couple of minutes along, turn right (signpost). Cross a track and, a few minutes later, cross the road to San Isidro by a building (2h35min; signpost: Mazo, PR LP17). Continue on the path that first veers sharply right and then left (by an enormous pine). After five minutes, join the Mazo track. Turn right and, after 20m/yds, turn left down a path (signpost). Cross a wooden bridge and rejoin the track. Turn left and, after 100m/yds, turn left again (signpost; 2h45min), immediately passing behind a shed, a house and another shed. Pass a viewpoint and, one minute later, at a junction, take the path going left (signpost). At a signposted crossing of paths, go straight on. Next, cross a minor track, only to rejoin it a minute later and follow it downhill. Another track now joins from the right. Almost immediately, at a T-junction, turn right (waymark). Pass a signpost after a few minutes and after another few minutes descend to an intersection of four tracks, where you turn left on a path (signpost). Ignore any faint turn-offs or tracks until, after five minutes, you pass an apple orchard and join a track (signpost). Follow the track to the right for 150m/yds, then turn onto the path again. The path crosses several tracks in the next 15 minutes (sometimes joining the track for 10 or 20m/yds; each junction is signposted or waymarked). When the path eventually widens into a track, turn right down to the road to the old Mazo dump (signpost; 3h40min). Turn left here and, when you reach the gates to the dump, descend to the right on a path. At the next track crossing, turn left (signpost) to pick up the continuing path. Twenty minutes later, cross a track and then a covered *canal*. Just below the *canal* you join a track and follow it downhill, crossing another track a minute later (signpost). The way finally joins a concrete lane, which you descend. On reaching a maze of country lanes, bear left after the third lane and descend a tarmac lane (signpost: Playa del Hoyo, PR LP17). The tarmac ends shortly; continue straight downhill on concrete. Cross a minor track and continue on the steep concreted track to the left of a

The Llano del Jable, a plain of pitch-black sand (Picnic 7c)

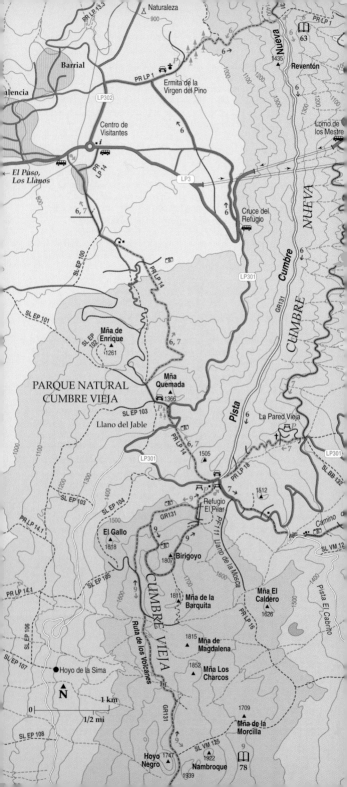

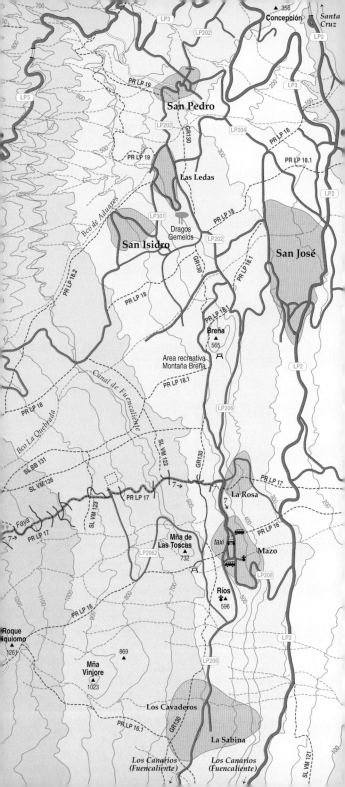

water tank. After a few minutes you arrive on the Mazo road in La Rosa (4h25min), just opposite a bus stop. Mazo is fifteen minutes along to the right. Keep right when you come to a fork in the road: the bus stop is just past the fork, and the taxi stand is a little further along (4h40min).

This walk is a good introduction to La Palma. Your views stretch across both the eastern and western slopes of the *cumbre*, the island's mountainous spine. And how different those two sides are: the north is verdant with woodlands, the south an intrigue of volcanic splendour with a desert of black sand.

Landscape beyond Montaña Quemada

Alight from the bus at the large lay-by east of the old tunnel on the LP3, at a place called **Lomo de los Mestres**. To **begin the walk**, head south on the forestry track by the tunnel entrance. Straight away you're engulfed by a dense mantle of trees and bushes. This evergreen forest, mainly composed of four types of laurel, covered much of southern Europe and North Africa some 15-40 million years ago. Unfortunately, little remains of this unique woodland, the Canary Islands and Madeira being its last refuge.

You snatch glimpses of San Pedro and some adjacent villages over the verdant slopes of the island's high eastern midriff. The only sounds will be birdsong and lizards torpedoing up the banks. After a gradual ascent you reach **La Pared Vieja**, a picnic area (**1h45min**; Picnic 7a). Apart from weekends, when it is very busy, this cool, shady *zona recreativa* makes a good resting place. (In 2009 and 2010 many pines were felled around here, and many others crashed down during storms in the last few years. This pine *(Pinus insignis)* was introduced by General Franco, but has proven too weak to stand the occasional winter storms because of its very shallow roots.)

First pass a track on the right, then a small building. Go straight ahead through the picnic area until you meet the El Pilar/San Isidro road (LP301). Don't follow it; instead, turn up to the right by a large information board and a sign, 'PARQUE NATURAL', and follow an old cobbled trail with yellow and white PR waymarks that passes above and to the left of the picnic area. Ignore small side paths and a track coming in from the left. Some 15m/yds further on you join a track coming from the right. At a junction of tracks two minutes later, keep straight ahead along a path. Cross the track and again rejoin the old path, as it ascends to the left. You pass a shrine on the right immediately. The *camino* climbs steadily, threading its way through the canopy of trees and shrubs.

Some 25 minutes up from the road, the path leaves the canopy of trees and widens out. At a small junction, turn left uphill on another path (signpost: REFUGIO DEL PILAR, PR LP18). Another junction follows, keep left (SIGNPOST). Volcanic mounds begin appearing through the trees. A shallow V in the ridge leads you up to an earthen track — the **Pista Cumbre Nueva** (**2h20min**; SIGNPOST). Turn left along this track. *(The Short walk begins here, and Alternative walk 6-1 joins here.)* Then turn right down the El Pilar road, past the **Refugio El Pilar** picnic area (Picnic 7b). *(But for the Alternative walk, turn left up this road, towards San Isidro.)*

Just opposite the main entrance to the *refugio* (which has a modest visitors' centre), turn right (sign on a tree, 'ACAMPADA', indicating a camping ground). Keep to the left of the showers and a shallow gully; after 50m/yds you will come upon a beautiful old waymarked path between the pines. After 15 minutes you come out of the trees into a stunning volcanic landscape, with magnificent views of the *caldera*. Cross the road (signpost, 'PR LP14, EL PASO, TACANDE') and continue on the path, beginning your descent to **Montaña Quemada** — the prominent grey-brown volcanic cone seen to your right.

When you meet the road again, don't follow it. Turn left onto the **Llano del Jable** and follow the main track for 200m/yds, then turn right on another track (signpost: 'EL PASO, PR LP14'). After another 300m/yds, at a junction of tracks, turn right (signpost: PR LP14, EL PASO; **2h50min**). Your path now crosses the tremendous lava flow from Montaña Quemada, which is just over 500 years old. On both sides are large lumps of volcanic rock covered in white and green lichen. After 10 minutes, near the end of Montaña Quemada, the path veers sharply left (SIGNPOST). Soon you reach the edge of the pine forest. The path does not enter it, but keeps following the lava downhill.

'Go with the flow' for the next 15 minutes, until the path gets steeper and zigzags down the lava, just before veering sharply right and leaving the flow. Climb for a minute, then continue downhill again. Ten minutes later, beautiful old stone walls appear on the right and a tremendous view opens up: the Cumbrecita in the distance and the Cumbre Nueva to the right. Some 50/yds further on, cross a track (SIGNPOST). The path is now flanked with old stone walls on both sides for the next 15 minutes. You pass a high fence and some houses on your right, and meet a road a minute later (SIGNPOST).

Follow the road to the right for 200m/yds and, at a signposted junction, descend the track straight ahead, lined with garden plots, orchards and some pretty houses. Ignore all side tracks and paths. When you meet the road again (**4h**), turn left. Five minutes later turn right on a waymarked track ('CENTRO VISITANTES CALDERA DE TABURIENTE'). Pass a few houses and come into the lava stream again. In 10 minutes you reach the main road. The **Visitors' Centre** is opposite and the BUS STOP and a restaurant 30m/yds to the right (**4h10min**).

Walk 8: LOS CANARIOS (FUENCALIENTE) • VOLCAN DE SAN ANTONIO • VOLCAN DE TENEGUIA • FARO DE FUENCALIENTE

See also photograph pages 22-23

Distance/time: 8km/5mi; 1h50min (16km/10mi; 4h20min if you return the same way)

Grade: moderate, with a descent of 700m/2300ft on gravel slopes (steep and stony in places). You must be sure-footed and have a head for heights, but this walk is *recommended for everyone* (there is only one very short stretch that might prove unnerving for those who suffer from vertigo). It is usually very windy here, especially around the volcanoes. Don't ascend to the rim of the Volcán de Teneguía in strong winds! *Red and white GR waymarking for most of the way*

Note: There is a pay booth at the Volcán de San Antonio, € 5 entry fee at press date; some walkers avoid this by going straight onto the path on the right, 100m/yds before the pay booth.

Equipment: walking boots, sunhat, sunglasses, suncream, long trousers, cardigan, anorak, raingear, swimwear, picnic, plenty of water

How to get there: 🚌 from Los Llanos or Santa Cruz to Los Canarios (Línea 3); journey time 35-40min

To return: 🚌 from El Faro to Los Canarios (Línea 31); journey time 35-40min, then 🚌 to Santa Cruz or Los Llanos as above (Línea 3).

Short walk: Volcán de San Antonio — Roque Teneguía — Volcán de Teneguía — Volcán de San Antonio (6km/3.5mi; 1h40min). Easy, but there is a stiff climb of 200m/650ft at the end. Equipment as above, but stout shoes will suffice. Access by 🚗: park at the Volcán de San Antonio (leave Los Canarios on the Las Indias road and, just past the last houses, turn left on a gravel track to the car park (fee payable). Follow the main walk from the 10min-point to the 1h05min-point, then return.

T he Volcán de Teneguía is one of the most colourful volcanoes on La Palma, and the combination of striking coastal scenery and intriguing volcanic landscape make this a 'not to be missed' hike — and exceedingly popular. The walk ends at Faro de Fuencaliente, a working fishing hamlet.

Begin the walk at the Bar Parada in **Los Canarios** (it's 200m/yds west of the bus stop on the main road). Walk down the narrow street opposite the bar. Go through a junction and reach the Las Indias road. Follow this to the right downhill and, after 100m/yds fork right on a road, the Calle de Los Volcanes. (This fork is just beyond the turn-off for the Bodega Teneguía visited in Car tour 2.) You pass an *urbanización* on the right. Descending, you look straight onto the dark, flat-topped **Volcán de San Antonio**. Cross the Las Indias road again and head straight on for the crater. There is a pay booth; the entry fee allows you to walk on the rim of the crater and visit the centre with a film about the Volcán San Antonio and the eruption of Teneguia in 1971. Go through the **Visitors' Centre** and onto the path at the

73

right-hand side of the volcano (**10min**). (*The Short walk starts here.*) A spectacular view opens up across hillside vineyards to Las Indias on your right; the sheer slopes of the western escarpment fill the backdrop, and you can see Puerto Naos, a handful of buildings backing onto a sea-flat of banana plantations. The crater rim is narrow in places, and some people may find a short stretch vertiginous. (Please don't lean on the 'safety ropes': you may end up in the crater...) Roque Teneguía is the yellow rock jutting out of the hillside below. The southern coast unfolds, with El Faro sitting near the southernmost tip, by glaring-white salt pans. But it's the magically-coloured Volcán de Teneguía that holds your gaze. It used to be possible to circle the whole crater on this path, but today it has been closed off halfway round for conservation reasons, so you will have to retrace your steps.

Return to the VISITORS' CENTRE, pass the pay booth and after 100m/yds turn left on a path (sign: FARO DE FUENCALIENTE, GR131). A steep, gravelly and dusty descent brings you down to a track: turn left. Rounding the slopes, you look down on Roque Teneguía. Banana plantations and greenhouses vie to smother the coastal flat. Barely five minutes along the track, fork right on a clear path down to **Roque Teneguía** (**50min**). Although not large, this hunk of rock is a prominent landmark and a good view-point. While you are here, look out for petroglyphs; there are several of them on the sloping side of the rock, but they are quite faded. A barrier prevents visitors from clambering over this fragile rock and damaging the petroglyphs even more.

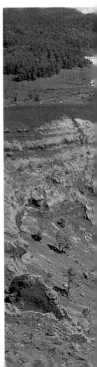

To continue, take the stone-marked path opposite the rock for three minutes, climb down into a gully and walk down until you reach the *canal*. Turn left along the *canal*. Shiny-leafed *vinagrera* (of the dock family) flourishes here. After a few minutes, descend to a track seen below (to the left of a large WATER TANK) and follow it to the left, towards the volcano. Then take a path off right, to the edge of the **Volcán de Teneguía** (**1h05min**).

(A path ascends the left-hand rim of this spectacularly-coloured crater. It's a stupendous climb, *but narrow, vertiginous*

Top: smooth rolling slopes on the descent to the lighthouse.
Middle: Roque Teneguía.
Bottom: the Volcán de San Antonio, with Los Canarios in the background

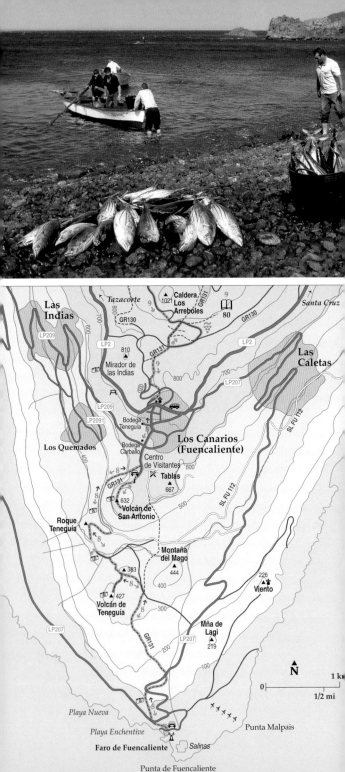

Above: descending to the lighthouse; left: at the beach

and very dangerous in a strong wind. If it's calm and you make this ascent, add 20 minutes. Inside the crater, holes in the left-hand wall emit hot gases.)

The main walk continues by retracing the path for barely a minute, to a bend. Here descend a waymarked path to the right, down into the lava. Keep between Teneguía and its offspring (a baby volcano) on the left. A clear path soon leads you to a junction, where you turn right. Within minutes, at another junction, turn right again on a cleared path through an intriguing lava stream. The twisted and jagged rock here is spellbinding.

Out of the lava stream, your path crosses smooth rolling slopes. As you mount a crest, the pink-tinted salt pans and the lighthouse appear not far below. On arriving at the ROAD TO THE LIGHTHOUSE (**1h35min**; SIGNPOST), turn right for 100m/yds, then pick up the continuation of your path on the left (SIGNPOST). A few minutes later cross the road again (SIGNPOST). Close to the edge of the cliffs, you look out over Playa Nueva, embraced by a lava flow.

Cross the road once more and descend to the tiny fishing hamlet of **Faro de Fuencaliente** (**1h50min**). It's a desolate yet striking spot. Parched, windswept and covered in dust, you're just in the mood for a dip, then a cool beer and a reviving meal in the new theme restaurant 'Jardin de la sal' right in the middle of the salt pans. There's a small but interesting marine reserve visitors' centre here, too, in the old lighthouse (free entry). There's a bus back to the village and a sign with the local taxi telephone

Walk 9: RUTA DE LOS VOLCANES

Map begins below and ends on page 80

Distance/time: 18km/11.25mi; 6h10min

Grade: fairly strenuous: although the ascent is only 500m/1600ft, the walk is very long, and much of it crosses volcanic gravel. Recommended only in fine weather: when the Cumbre Vieja is under cloud or mist, it's very easy to stray off the path, and *this could be dangerous.* Can be cold and windy. One short stretch demands a head for heights. *Red and white GR waymarking; some green and white SL waymarking*

Equipment: walking boots, sunhat, sunglasses, suncream, raingear, warm cardigan, anorak, picnic, plenty of water

How to get there: 🚕 taxi or with friends to the Refugio El Pilar
To return: 🚌 from Los Canarios to Santa Cruz or Los Llanos (Línea 3); journey time 35-40min

Shorter walk: El Pilar — Volcán Deseada — El Pilar (13km/8.1mi; 3h50min). Grade, equipment and access as main walk. Follow the main walk to the 2h15min-point and return the same way.

Short circular walk: Birigoyo — or Ruta de los Volcanes 'lite' (4.5km/2.8mi; 1h50min). This short, but very pretty walk, with tremendous views, is the best option if you don't have time or stamina for the whole Ruta de los Volcanes. Grade: moderate, but with an ascent and descent of 350m/1150ft on gravelly, loose rock and sand. Take a walking stick! Follow the main walk for 25 minutes, then turn left on a path signposted 'Birigoyo'. Follow this up to the rim of the volcano and look into the impressive crater (35min). Now turn right on a path marked with cairns, which rounds the crater on the south side. On this stiff climb you enjoy tremendous views to the south, east and west — if the weather is clear you can see both coasts. Climbing higher, round the crater towards

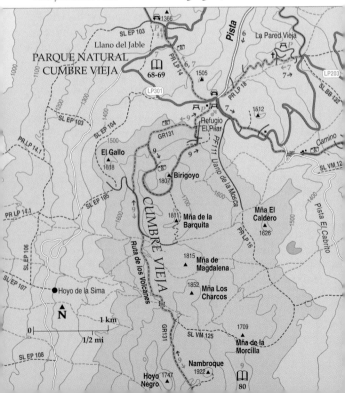

the north, ignoring some minor paths to the right and always keeping to the crater rim. From the summit of Birigoyo (1h05min) there's an uninterrupted view over the Caldera de Taburiente — better than from any vantage point on the Ruta de los Volcanes. A steep zigzag descent over loose terrain follows, past a smaller crater on the right. On reaching the first shrubs (1h20min) the path veers to the right and zigzags down into the forest (1h30min). Five minutes later first ignore a small trail to the left, then turn left down a large firebreak, ignoring a track on the left. Just 100m/yds further down another track crosses the fire break; follow this to the left. It narrows to a path. Keeping straight on, you meet your outgoing path a minute later. Follow it to the right for less than 10 minutes, back to the Refugio del Pilar (1h50min).

Other short walks from the Refugio El Pilar: see these suggestions on page 66.

Here's a walk to rival Tenerife's Cañadas or Lanzarote's Timanfaya. You go from one volcano to another, and each is more impressive than the last. Magnificent views lure you on, surround you, and trail behind you. By the time you reach Los Canarios, you'll have seen enough volcanoes to last a lifetime.

The walk starts by the VISITORS' CENTRE in the **Refugio El Pilar** picnic area (Picnic 7b). Some 50m/yds beyond (south of) this building, turn right on a path opposite a WATER TANK (signpost: LOS CANARIOS, GR131). A steep ascent up through a pine wood follows. Under 10 minutes uphill, at a fork, keep right. Soon you're following a well-manicured path around the steep slopes of a volcano. Leaving the pines, a fine panorama unfolds at a *mirador* with a signboard (**15min**): the hillsides slide down into the pine-studded basin cradling the Llano del Jable. Beyond these dark sands lie grassy fields, below the walls of the crater and the *cumbre*. El Paso spreads around the tail of a lava tongue, and Los Llanos is swallowed up amidst banana plantations.

Walk round the hillside, ignoring any paths ascending to the left *(but take the 'Birigoyo' path for the Short circular walk)*. Descend to a TRACK (**45min**; SIGNPOST). Turn left uphill, ignoring some minor tracks and paths. Then, after 15 minutes, turn right on a wide path (initially flanked by stone walls; SIGNPOST), into a 'rock garden' of *codeso (Adenocarpus)* and chrysanthemums.

Cross a WOODEN BRIDGE (**1h20min**) and, a good five minutes later, ignore two paths to the left (SIGNPOST). After another 10 minutes' climbing, you reach a jagged-edged crater on the right. This is **Hoyo Negro** (the 'black hollow'), looking exactly like its name. Ten minutes later, you're peering down into a lava lake, the **Cráter del Duraznero** (**1h55min**). Descend to the right of this cone

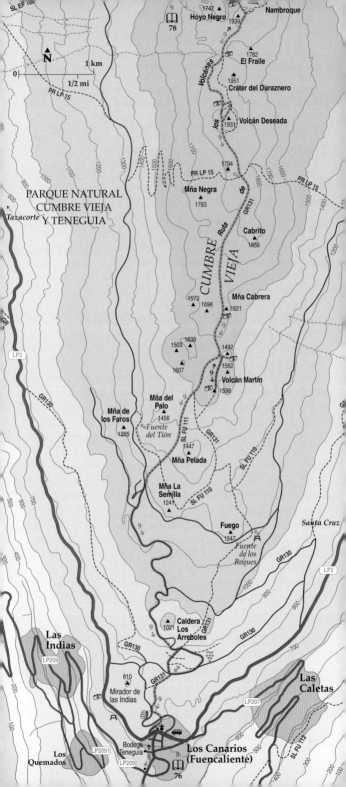

Left: climbing above the Refugio El Pilar at the start of the walk. Right: looking back along the route, not far beyond Volcán Deseada. Below: at 3h10min the best views on the hike unfold, when Volcán Martín is seen ahead.

and, after a few minutes, at a fork, turn left uphill. (You will rejoin the right-hand fork further on.) Just below the edge of the brilliantly-coloured **Volcán Deseada (2h15min)**, the path forks to encircle it. Take the right fork. A minute later the crater tumbles away below you. Stay on the higher path halfway round the crater. A twin crater, to the left of the main one, emanates equally striking pastel hues — orange, pink, yellow and cream. (*The Shorter walk returns from here.*)

Leaving Deseada, you mount a neck of ridge, and ascend to yet another crater (**2h35min**). There are several paths to the rim of the crater — any one will do. This crater offers a spectacular view along the volcanic spine of its dark naked slopes. Swifts by the score whistle past. Bearing round to the right, you pass a CONCRETE POST. Just below the post, you rejoin the path that forked right just beyond El Duraznero. Continue straight downhill here. Leaving a shallow basin (SIGNPOST), you cross a low crest. At a crossroads of paths (SIGNPOST; there is a WATER TAP 20m/yds to your right) carry straight on. Entering a long shallow valley (**3h10min**), head across the sand and continue straight downhill (SIGNPOST); the odd survey post and stones intermittently line the path.

Soon (**3h45min**) the best views of the hike unfold (INFORMATION BOARD). The sea appears just over the edge of the sandy volcanic slopes, with the reddish-pink cone of Volcán Martín stealing the show. Luminous green pines dot the immediate hillsides. Within 10 minutes, at a major fork on the slopes of **Volcán Martín** (**4h**; SIGNPOST), turn left. Turn left again at the fork that follows immediately. A minute downhill you're looking straight down into Volcán Martín, its rim ablaze with shades of mauve, cream and orange. Opposite, you can see a spring in a cave beside the crater floor. This is your last volcano, I promise.

Return to the forks and take the second left. (Or, if you're a glutton for punishment, take the first left, to ascend the crater rim and take in the extravaganza of

'Gluttons for punishment' can take a 15-minute detour along the rim of Volcán Martín to enjoy this extravaganza of volcanic hues.

volcanic hues shown above — as well as a good view over the southern tip of the island. Allow an extra 15 minutes for this.) Continuing, just head straight downhill, ploughing down through the fine gravel — great fun. Just below Volcán Martín turn right at a fork, *leaving* the main GR131 path for another well-trodden path with green and white SL waymarking (signpost, 'FUENTE DEL TION').

When you reach a TRACK (**4h35min**), cross it (signpost: LOS CANARIOS POR PISTA). Then descend for a few minutes, to a junction (SIGNPOST). Take the track opposite and, from now on, just follow the signs for 'LOS CANARIOS' — going right at a fork after about 30 minutes (signpost: 'LOS ARREBOLES, FUENCALIENTE'). (After about 55 minutes the track crosses the original GR131 footpath to Los Canarios. If you decide to take this short-cut, turn right here. After three minutes cross another footpath and after another few minutes cross the track, to continue along the path, rejoining the main walk.)

Attention is needed around 1h down the main track (**5h40min**), when you are circling to the right of a vineyard. Just before it, ignore a minor turn-off left. After a few minutes a track joins you from the left. Ignore the signposted path to the right, and continue on the track towards Los Canarios. A few minutes later, keep an eye out for a WATER TANK on the right. Some 30m/yds past the tank, turn left on a path (signpost: 'GR131') and follow it straight downhill, picking up red and white waymarking again.

On reaching a road, follow it to the left (SIGNPOST). Soon you pass a basin with pines and see a sports field in the distance. Where the road veers right, take the path to the left (SIGNPOST). Los Canarios comes into sight just below, through the trees. On meeting the road again, cross it and continue on the path (SIGNPOST). Emerging on a street in **Los Canarios** (**6h05min**), follow it 100m/yds downhill to the MAIN ROAD. Turn left and walk past Bar Parada (where Walk 8 begins). THE BUS STOP is just three minutes further on; a bus shelter is opposite (**6h10min**).

Walk 10: PICO BEJENADO

See also photograph page 6   **Distance:** 12.5km/8mi; 4h25min

Grade: strenuous, with an ascent/descent of 700m/2300ft, but suitable for anyone who is reasonably fit. You must be sure-footed, and a few stretches demand a head for heights. Only suitable in fine weather; should clouds descend, the utmost care needed, especially at the summit. If a strong wind is blowing, keep away from rim of the crater. Signposting and yellow/white waymarking (PR LP13,3).

Equipment: walking boots, sunhat, sunglasses, suncream, raingear, long-sleeved shirt, long trousers, warm cardigan, warm jacket, gloves, picnic, plenty of water

How to get there and return: 🚗 car to/from El Barrial, above Valencia. Turn off the El Paso/Santa Cruz LP3 road for 'Parque Nacional' (at the visitor centre). Keep straight on at the first junction but, shortly after, turn left for Valencia. Keep ahead on this road for 3.3km and park when it reverts to rough track. (Another parking area lies further up this track, at the point where the ascent proper begins and the road is once again surfaced; you may prefer to park there if you are in a 4WD vehicle.)

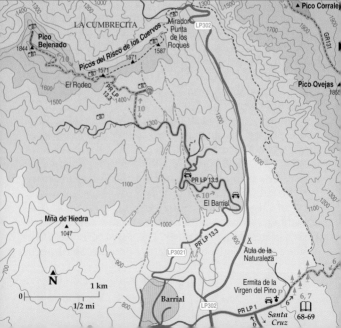

Pico Bejenado, like Pico de la Nieve, is accessible to everyone, and for this reason alone, worth the effort of the ascent. You'll feel like an eagle once on the summit, as you peer down into every corner of the Caldera de Taburiente (Walk 11). And on the ascent you have a sweeping vista over the Los Llanos basin as it spills out into the sea. This hike offers a superlative of views.

These timings begin at the point where the asphalt *first* ends (sign: 'PR LP13,3 BEJENADO'). Follow the track ahead to the turn-off for the ascent, by a large park INFORMATION BOARD and a second parking area with SIGNPOST (**20min**). Ignore a track to the right and one to the left at the outset. At a junction (**35min**) go left ('PICO BEJENADO, POR PETROGLIFO, 4900M'). Ignore a wide path ascending to the right just past the junction. The hillsides are wooded in Canary pines and bare of undergrowth. Pico Bejenado is the peak furthest to the left in the wall of mountains ahead.

Another SIGN (**1h**) points your way up a wide path to the right. (A curiosity: there's a rubbish bin here with braille lettering.) The path ascends beside a large fenced-off area, where they are trying to recover some almost extinct indigenous plants. Minutes up, the path narrows and zigzags. A little over five minutes later, keep left at a fork (sign: PETROGLIFOS 150M). But it's worth taking the short detour to right, to see the large petroglyph and take in the excellent views over the mountains near La Cumbre-cita. The ascent steepens as you mount the shoulder of the crater, but the panorama expands to encompass the west coast, where a gentle built-up plain fans out from the basin of fields tucked back into the *cumbre*.

Ignore a path to the left (**1h35min**). Soon the rim of the crater is just before you (**1h45min**). Go left (SIGN); the path to the right leads to La Cumbrecita. The far walls of the pine-speckled *caldera* below you may well be under a mantle of clouds, which only enhances the picture (as in the photograph opposite). This is **El Rodeo** (SIGNPOST).

Finally, you reach the summit of **Pico Bejenado** (**2h 25min**), with a bird's-eye view over the whole crater, lined by streams of ridges pouring down off the encircling wall of mountains. The strip of *barranco* bed visible below is the Playa de Taburiente. If you scramble down the 2m/6ft-high rock-face on the west side of the summit and continue to the end of the ridge, you will be able to look down into the Barranco de las Angustias and trace the forestry track up its far wall to Los Brecitos, where Walk 11 begins.

Retrace your steps to the LOWER CAR PARK (**4h25min**).

Distance/time: 13.5km/8.4mi; 5h

Grade: long and quite strenuous, with a descent of 850m/2790ft, but accessible to all fit walkers who are sure-footed and have a head for heights. *Don't attempt in bad or windy weather, or after heavy rain:* conditions change every year in the *barranco* after heavy rainfall, with a danger of rockfall or (very rarely) flash flooding. The going also depends on how much water the *barranco* is carrying, making the walk easier (usually in summer) or more difficult (usually in winter). Other hints: It can be very cool: be prepared! And don't lean on any handrails: they may be loose. PR LP13 signposting; yellow/white waymarking

Important notes: Permission is needed from the Parques Nacionales if you intend to stay in the national park overnight (obtain this at the visitor centre on the LP3, or telephone 922-922280 or book online at http://www.reservas parquesnacioinales.es), and you may camp *only* at the designated site. *Please don't follow the watercourses in this crater, as suggested in some books: they are too dangerous — tourists have died as a result.*

Equipment: walking boots, sunhat, sunglasses, suncream, raingear, long-sleeved shirt, long trousers, warm cardigan, warm jacket, gloves, swimwear, picnic, water, walking stick. It's a good idea to leave a dry pair of shoes, socks and trousers in your car or backpack, especially in the winter, in case you slip while crossing the river!

How to get there and return: 🚗 car or taxi to/from the parking area in the floor of the Barranco de las Angustias (see Car tour 3, page 26), then jeep taxi to Los Brecitos (they wait here for walkers; shared cost is about 10 € per person). *Note:* the taxis only operate from 08.30-12.30

Short walk: Barranco de las Angustias (up to 5.5km/3.4mi; 1h50min). Grade, equipment, access and instructions as *Alternative walk*. Follow the *Alternative walk* to Morro de la Era (an ascent/descent of about 130m/425ft) — or turn back any time you like.

Alternative walk: Barranco de las Angustias — Cascada Colorada — Barranco de las Angustias (10.5km/6.5mi; 5h). Moderate, with an ascent/descent of some 250m/820ft; much clambering over rocks and some paddling. Equipment as main walk. Access as main walk, but no jeep taxi necessary. From the parking area in the floor of the Barranco de las Angustias simply follow the yellow and white PR LP13 waymarking and 'Zona de Acampada' signposting, to climb the bed of the *barranco*. Remain in this *barranco*, ignoring side-*barrancos* off to the left. This is the main walk in reverse; use the map to locate various landmarks. Beyond Dos Aguas, in the Barranco Río Almendro Amargo, be sure to keep to the right in the Barranco de Ribanseras. You will reach the waterfall shown on page 90 in under 3h. Remember that conditions in the *barranco* change every winter and you may have to paddle and or clamber over landslides to get to the waterfall.

The Caldera de Taburiente *is* La Palma. If you don't spend at least a day in it, you haven't really seen the island. Streams tumble down from every *barranco*; indeed, these streams formed the *caldera* (cauldron), which at first was thought to be volcanic. Some nine kilometres (six miles) across at its widest point, and 2000 metres (over a mile) deep, Taburiente is one of the largest craters in the world to be formed by erosion. Recent studies, however, shy away from the crater theory, claiming it to be a massive landslide instead. It's one of La Palma's three natural wonders (the other two being the Ruta de los Volcanes and Los Tilos).

The walk starts at the car park in **Los Brecitos**: descend the path by a large NATIONAL PARK SIGNBOARD, pass through a turnstile, and head down into the *caldera*. Follow the path signposted 'ZONA DE ACAMPADA', ignoring all turn-offs. Hillsides tumble away below, and the

Looking up the Barranco de Ribanseras del Castro from just below its confluence with the Río Almendro Amargo (Cruce de Barrancos)

rocky crater walls tower overhead, with pines clinging to the sheer slopes. *(Note that the pine needles are slippery underfoot.)* You cross a number of small *barrancos*, some with streams. The prominent peak rising out of the *caldera* wall opposite is Pico Bejenado. Walk 10 goes to its very top.

A large boulder marks your crossing of the **Barranco de las Traves** (**35min**). More boulders begin appearing on the hillsides. The next ravine, the **Barranco de las Piedras Redondas** ('ravine of round rocks'), is well-named. The **Mirador del Lomo de Tagasaste**, from where you have a good view into the centre of the crater, follows. The deeply-gouged ravine of the **Barranco de Bombas de Agua** (**1h15min**) will either impress you or terrify you, or both, as you continue along the path! Erosion here eats away at least a couple of feet from the *barranco* walls every year.

You finally arrive at the floor of the **Río Taburiente** at a wide basin known as the **Playa de Taburiente** (**1h 25min**). Here you're enveloped by grand scenery. Small clumps of cool, shady Canary willow (*Salix canariensis*) stretch along the wide stony *playa*, where you can paddle in smaller or larger pools with crystal-clear water.

To continue to the camping site, cross the river, hopping over boulders and stones, and look out for a gap in the willows on your right approximately 50m/yds downstream (SIGNPOST; WAYMARK), to locate the path that ascends the eastern bank of the river to the CAMPING SITE above (**1h30min**). There is an attractive stone-built services centre here (information and toilets).

Keep to the left of the buildings (SIGNPOST); follow a wide path over to

the edge of a cliff with a wonderful view straight down to the Río Taburiente. The path continues over a col and soon Roque Idafe comes into sight, a prominent finger of rock balancing on the end of a ridge.

The **Somada del Palo** (**1h45min**), a signposted viewpoint on a nose of hillside jutting out into the plunging **Barranco del Río Almendro Amargo** ('bitter almond'), provides a fine perch over the river and equally good views back up to the heights of the crater. After about 30 minutes' descent on the partly-cobbled, winding path, look back up the *barranco* for a good view of a wall spanning the ravine. At the fork that follows five minutes later, keep right. A few minutes later the path that

90

Facing page: path beyond the camping area above the Río Taburiente, not long before reaching the Somada del Palo (top); the orange-yellow rocks at the Cascada Colorada in the Barranco de Ribanseras del Castro owe their colour to the iron content in the river (bottom). Above: in the Barranco de las Angustias, near Morro de la Era

branched off to the left rejoins your route at **Las Lajitas del Viento**, from where you continue downhill.

Another signpost ('LAS ANGUSTIAS/ZONA DE ACAMPADA; **2h25min**), marks the confluence of two streams. *At this point you could make an optional 45 minute detour to the 'coloured waterfall'*: to get there, head left here (CAIRNS), scrambling down on all fours to the BED OF THE **Río Almendro Amargo**. Notice the rust-coloured water, caused by the high iron content. Follow this *barranco* to the left for a minute then, when it forks, continue to the right (noting the pretty waterfall on the left) and ascend to the bed of the **Barranco de Ribanseras del Castro**. (*Note:* this stream needs to be crossed several times on loose slippery rocks, and the last two minutes are awkward and need care.) In 15 minutes you arrive at the 'coloured waterfall' shown on page 90 (**Cascada Colorada**), a brilliant sight. Return the same way from the cascade, but remain in the bed of the *barranco,* keeping downstream below the path from Cruce de Barrancos.

The main walk continues along the path, reaching the river bed in five minutes. There is usually a fair amount of water here all year round, as no water is collected at this point. Hop across as best you can — with a bit of luck you'll keep dry! Soon you arrive at **Dos Aguas** (**2h40min**), the confluence of the Almendro Amargo and Taburiente gorges. There is a giant grate on the left here, to collect debris from the river where it flows into a *canal.* Cross the Río Taburiente, then pick up the continuing path (at the left of a low concrete wall built across the **Barranco de las Angustias**; signpost: 'BARRANCO DE LAS ANGUSTIAS, SALIDA'). Continue downstream along this *barranco.*

The time spent in the *barranco* greatly depends on your agility, as you scramble over rocks and jump across the river. Depending on the amount of water the river carries, you may have to leave the stream bed several times (all paths are signposted). The first detour is just after a large pipe crosses the *barranco* above your head (at about **3h10min**). The second comes up about five minutes later, on the left-hand wall. The third is also on the left. The fourth is on the *right-hand* wall. (Of course it is usually possible to stay in the bed of the *barranco,* getting your feet wet!)

Eventually you arrive at **Morro de la Era**, a derelict stone building (**3h50min**). After returning to the *barranco* for five minutes, there's another detour up the left wall, then you descend once more to the *barranco* bed (**4h15min**). Before crossing the stream again from here, head *upstream* for two minutes, to a delightful pool and cascade hidden in a rocky corridor under a natural rock arch — most hikers miss this spot. After a final detour up the right wall, continue in the stream bed, which eventually dries up (in summer). Then you arrive at the main track; your car will be in the PARKING AREA a couple of minutes along to the left (**5h**).

Walk 12: FROM THE MIRADOR EL TIME TO PUERTO DE TAZACORTE

Distance/time: 3km/2mi; 1h05min

Grade: easy but steep descent of 600m/2000ft; not suitable in wet weather. You should have a head for heights, but the path is generally quite wide. *Red and white GR waymarking*

Equipment: walking boots, sunhat, sunglasses, warm cardigan, water, bathing suit

How to get there: 🚌 bus from Los Llanos (Línea 2) to the Mirador El Time; journey time 25min
To return: 🚌 from Puerto de Tazacorte to Los Llanos (Línea 21); journey time 15min. Or return to Los Llanos on foot: follow the valley road for a little over 1km, to where signposting alerts you to the GR130 off right. Cross a footbridge and follow the red/white waymarked trail back to Los Llanos.

This walk is one long, continuous panorama. The vista stretches out over the Los Llanos plain and along the west coast to the south of the island. It's a short walk ideally done in the late afternoon, a great 'appetiser' for beginners.

Set out from the **Mirador El Time**, but first take in the superb panorama at this viewpoint. Small volcanic cinder cones stand out on the inclines, speckled with white houses, and banana plantations stretch for as far as the eye can see. The cliffs below you plunge down into the Barranco de las Angustias before it cleaves its way into the Caldera de Taburiente (Walk 11).

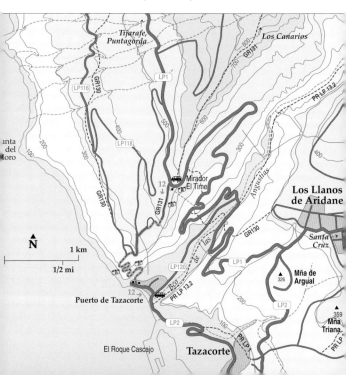

Walk downhill on the narrow road on the northwest side of the restaurant and souvenir shop (SIGNPOST). The hillside below you is stepped in banana groves all the way to the sea-cliffs. When you reach the EDGE OF THE CLIFFS (**5min**) an even more expansive view unfolds, all the way up the Barranco de las Angustias and into the Caldera de Taburiente.

A few minutes later, our way leads through walled-in banana groves. Leaving the groves on a rough track, go right to round the hillside, following the good GR waymarking. Another few minutes along, turn left downhill, to join a road and descend amidst greenhouses.

Descend to a T-junction and turn left (**20min**; signpost: 'GR131 PUERTO DE TAZACORTE'). Follow the road to the left, past park-sized gardens ablaze with colour and some ritzy homes enjoying a stupendous view. Three minutes down the road, turn left down a concrete ramp (SIGNPOST) which becomes a nicely cobbled path. After a few minutes on this path, flanked by high walls, the path joins the road again, next to an old banana-packing

94

From the old cobbled camino real you have a superb view over Puerto de Tazacorte, spectacularly located at the mouth of the Barranco de las Angustias.

station, before continuing downhill to the left (SIGN-POST).

From here you are walking into a picture-postcard. You edge along the rim of the plummeting Barranco de las Angustias, peering down onto Puerto de Tazacorte. From up here you can appreciate its beautiful location at the mouth of the *barranco*. On reaching the sea-cliffs, the way twists and winds down the sheer face of the escarpment. Don't walk *too* near the edge, as the cliffs drop away without warning ... you might do the same! The descent is made even more impressive because of the beautifully-made path underfoot — an old cobbled *camino real*, which descends in zigzags. Offshore you can see some large fish cages (fish farming), and the colourful village lies below you in the mouth of the *barranco*.

About half way down the cliffs (**40min**), the route veers left across the wall of the *barranco*. A bit further down you pass a number of once-inhabited caves, now barred up to prevent hippies from using them. You finally approach the port from behind banana groves (beware of broken glass here). You enter **Puerto de Tazacorte** (**1h05min**) between two restaurants. Walk along the promenade for 100m, then turn left into Calle Explanada and round the plaza. Then bear right to the CASA DEL MAR BUS STOP.

Walk 13: TIJARAFE • PORIS DE CANDELARIA • TIJARAFE

Distance: 5.5km/3.5mi; 3h05min

Grade: very strenuous, with a descent/reascent of 650m/2100ft. You must be sure-footed and have a head for heights. Don't attempt in wet or windy weather. Although people *do* swim at Poris de Candelaria, I would not generally recommend it because of the swell. *Yellow and white PR waymarking near the coast; higher up, follow the cairns carefully!*

Equipment: walking boots, sunhat, sunglasses, suncream, warm cardigan, raingear, swimwear (just in case the sea is mirror-calm), picnic, plenty of water

How to get there and return: 🚌 from Los Llanos to/from Tijarafe (Línea 2); journey time about 45min. Or 🚗: park in Tijarafe and make your way to the Supermercado San Antonio and the kiosk on the main LP1 road.

Alternative return to Tijarafe: After visiting Poris de Candelaria, go back to the 1h10min-point and take the narrow concrete road back up to Tijarafe. The time is approximately the same, but the ascent is easier.

Poris de Candelaria is an exquisite little hideaway. Supposedly, it was once used for just that purpose by pirates. Although there is a motorable lane down to this little cove, most drivers would find it far too hair-raising. If you're really fit, a far better way to get there is on foot, following this brilliant, if strenuous walk.

Start out in **Tijarafe**. From the BUS STOP, cross the street, walk uphill to the SUPERMERCADO SAN ANTONIO and the little KIOSK next to the AYUNTAMIENTO and take the road between them. Passing between the GUARDIA CIVIL and the CENTRO DE SALUD, the street narrows into a concrete lane and descends steeply, flanked by terraced plots.

At an INTERSECTION (**10min**), turn right on a track. Three minutes along, where the track bends right, turn left on a minor path. The path leads down alongside a rocky crest, with a *barranco* falling away on the left. Lone pines

Right: coastal view about an hour downhill. Below: descending to the 'pirates' cove (left); heading into the cove itself, where weekend retreats are built into the massive rock overhang.

dot the grassy inclines. *Watch carefully* now for the small CAIRNS that waymark the route; this crest is criss-crossed with goat paths — all of which look like potential footpaths!

On coming abreast of a GREENHOUSE on the opposite crest to the left (**25min**), the way forks. Go left (the paths rejoin, but the path to the left is much easier to follow). The path bends sharp left very briefly, then it keeps straight down the crest. The trail disappears from time to time, so *needs attention:* keep your eye out for the cairns. After about five minutes along the top of the ridge, the path descends the right-hand side of the crest, but without crossing the shallow *barranco* on the right. As you head steeply down over bedrock, move from cairn to cairn. A mixture of vegetation grows out of the grass: *tabaiba, taginaste, vinagrera, verode* and prickly pear.

You meet a cobbled path above a DRY CASCADE (**40min** or more, depending on your navigational skills), looking down over the rugged coastline. Go left and descend a little, finally crossing the *barranco* below the cascade. Follow this path zigzagging down the steep slopes. The path is wide, but may still be unnerving for inexperienced hikers. Loose stones and gravel make this steep descent slippery, so take your time.

Ten minutes below the cascade, the path passes very

close to the top of a cliff from where there is an excellent view across the plunging sea-cliffs to the northwest coast. Large clumps of the cactus-like candelabra spurge begin appearing on the seaward slopes. A number of small caves lie beside the path; nearer the shore many have been converted into sheds.

A path coming from the narrow concrete road and parking area joins your path (**1h10min**), and from here the good wide path shown on page 96 takes you down into the hidden cove, **Poris de Candelaria** (**1h15min**). Rounding the point, the most unexpected sight appears: an enormous shallow sea cave towers overhead. Weekend retreats, dwarfed by the 50m/150ft-high overhang, huddle around its base, just at the edge of this tiny inlet.

The bad news is: the homeward leg is 1h50min of sweat and tears. The good news is: when you reach **Tijarafe** (**3h05min**), beer will never have tasted better!

Walk 14: FROM TIJARAFE TO TINIZARA

See map opposite   **Distance/time:** 6km/3.5mi; 2h15min
Grade: easy-moderate, with ascents of about 300m/1000ft overall. *Red and white GR waymarking for most of the way*
Equipment: walking boots, sunhat, sunglasses, suncream, warm cardigan, raingear, picnic, plenty of water
How to get there: 🚌 from Los Llanos (Línea 2); alight one stop beyond Tijarafe village; journey time about 45min
To return: 🚌 same bus from Tinizara; journey time about 55min

My hiking companions call this the 'friendly hike', and so it is. Following bits and pieces of the *camino real* along the cultivated western shelf of La Palma, you seem to pass through everyone's back garden. The proud old cobbled trails weave their way amidst terraced plots of almond trees and dip into ravines in between them.

In the bus push the button, or shout 'Para aquí por favor', just after you pass the main part of the village of **Tijarafe** and a big bend in the road. **The walk begins** just northwest of the BUS STOP, some 50m/yds uphill from SUPERMERCADO CANDELARIA. Turn left down a road and then take the first right, heading through fields of almond trees with strips of vineyards and clumps of prickly pear in their midst. After two minutes, when the road swings left, turn right on a track (signpost: PUNTAGORDA, GR130, CAMINO REAL DE LA COSTA). Then turn left on a cobbled trail, rejoining the road one minute later (SIGNPOST). Now follow the road downhill. Palm trees begin appearing, dotting the landscape. The terrain is very rocky, with many ravines concealed in the inclines. After two minutes, when the road curves left to descend the *barranco*, turn right (SIGNPOST) to climb the ravine on the old *camino*.

Soon (**10min**), flanked by an extravaganza of flowers, opposite a house, you meet a road. Cross straight over onto a path flanked by a high stone wall. Round the hillside on a clear path through almond groves, ignoring side paths. Seven minutes past the house, ignore a fork to the right, and immediately cross the **Barranco de la Cueva Grande**. Climb a splendid piece of old trail, and then emerge on a road, at a bend. Turn left downhill (SIGNPOST).

At a junction two minutes down the road (where there is a WATER TANK on the left), keep straight ahead on a concrete track (**25min**; SIGNPOST). Pass a SHRINE on your right and, 50m/yds further on, come to a house. Continue to the right of this house, surrounded by other beautiful, newly-built houses. Now the descent begins into the picturesque **Barranco del Pinillo**, where there is a gigantic rocky protrusion in the ravine wall and a large house built partly in the rock. Not far downhill, turn left on a path (SIGNPOST) and follow it down to the floor of the *barranco*. Creepers drape the ravine walls. On your ascent up the other side, both abandoned and renovated houses lie along the route.

Cross another (tiny) stream bed and soon pass a beautifully restored house (**45min**). Just after it, you come to two houses just above a road: climb the steps between them and head straight up the hillside on a path. You touch on a track for just 10m.yds, then continue to the right on the faint and overgrown cobbled path with the water pipes alongside it. Soon you pass by a renovated rustic

Opposite: ascending to Tinizara on the camino real, *the old stone-laid trail.
Above: attractive house with shrine*

homestead. On reaching the road again, in front of a large
Canary palm, follow it downhill to the left, but don't forget
to look back occasionally, over the green hillsides
descending to the sea, speckled with dark soldier-straight
pines. In the distance lies the chain of volcanoes that
punctures the island's southern spine.

Rounding a bend, about five minutes down the road,
you'll see another palm tree on the right. Turn right into
this track, despite the sign 'PISTA PRIVADA'. Pass a house
and, 50m/yds further on, another house. Go close to the
right-hand side of the garage belonging to the second
house, then turn left and continue from here on the barely-
visible path behind the house, descending over bare rock.
You reach a road in a few minutes. Turn right on the road,
into the ravine, where you come upon a lone pine on the
left. Branch off left by this tree (SIGNPOST) on a trail that
cuts down into the stream bed. You are on the *camino real*
once more. At the fork a minute downhill, turn right
uphill. A minute up, you come onto a concrete lane, just
as it becomes tarmac (SIGNPOST). Follow this downhill.

Rounding the hillside, you cross another small ravine.
At the SIGNPOST, turn right on a cobbled path. Small stone
dwellings sit partially hidden in the rocky terrain,
camouflaged by clumps of prickly pear cactus. Note the
white powder on the prickly pear. It's the cochineal
parasite, which used to be collected for its scarlet dye. After
a minute along the path, turn right uphill to a road
(**1h15min**; SIGNPOST). Pass tracks to your left and right,
and pass the charming early 19th-century house shown
above (on your right). Notice the shrine in the wall. A

The ascent from the Barranco de la Baranda to Tinizara is the most picturesque stretch of the walk.

minute later the GR130 turns off left, only to reach the road again three minutes later. Follow the road for 100m/yds, then branch off right (SIGNPOST). Climb up the hill on his beautiful old footpath and when you meet the road again 10 minutes later, cross it. Soon you reach the edge of a big ravine, the **Barranco de la Baranda**. The trail drops you down into a chasm — the deepest of them all, and a fine shady place to picnic. Cross a stream bed overgrown with blackberry bushes.

From here, the way to Tinizara is a steep climb, but the most picturesque section of the walk, up the fine old trail shown on page 100 (ignore all side-paths; continue straight up). Almonds wood the terraced hillsides. Just below the ROAD (**2h05min**), you pass a handful of houses — some traditional, some new, some renovated. Cross the road (SIGNPOST) and continue on the path. A minute up, reach the road again. Follow it to the left. After two minutes, turn up a wide path to the LP1 (SIGNPOST). The BUS STOP in **Tinizara** (**2h15min**) lies 50m/yds to the left. The local bar is a minute further along.

Walk 15: EL FAYAL • LAS TRICIAS • CUEVAS DE BURACAS • LAS TRICIAS

See also photograph page 2

Distance: 6.25km/4mi; 2h35min (2h05min for motorists)

Grade: relatively easy, with a descent of 400m/1300ft and ascent of 300m/1000ft. You must be sure-footed and have a head for heights. Not recommended in wet weather. *Red and white GR waymarking, also local waymarking with wooden signs*

Equipment: walking boots, sunhat, sunglasses, suncream, warm cardigan, picnic, plenty of water

How to get there: 🚌 from Los Llanos to the turn-off for the El Fayal *zona recreativa* just beyond Puntagorda (Línea 2); journey time about 1h15min. Or 🚗: park in Las Tricias and use the map to join the walk at the 45min-point, less than 15min away, saving 30 minutes.
To return: 🚌 from Las Tricias to Los Llanos (Línea 2); same journey time

Las Tricias is known for two groups of residents — arboreal (the unique assembly of dragon trees) and human (the transient 'alternative life-stylers'). Both have become noteworthy curiosities in themselves, attracting tourists in droves. To avoid the crush, finish this walk before midday, and you'll be able to share the sights with just a few other people.

Begin the walk from the BUS STOP AT THE TURN-OFF FOR EL FAYAL: continue north along the road towards Las Tricias. The surrounding slopes are wooded in Canary pines. Three minutes along, you'll see a LARGE INFORMATION BOARD and signposting for SANTO DOMINGO at the side of the road and a small white SHRINE below you, on the edge of the Barranco de Izcagua. Take the path down past the shrine and into the *barranco* (signposting: LAS TRICIAS). The path sidles down the sheer escarpment, where some guard rails lend psychological support *(but don't lean on them!)*. A stand of pine trees fills the valley floor. Ten minutes down, the way swings left and enters the bed of the **Barranco de Izcagua**. Five metres further on, the path leaves it again, to ascend the right-hand bank.

Mount the crest, greeted by a grove of almond trees. Continuing along the edge of the *barranco*, pass through a gate (please leave it as you find it) and ignore a few entrances to fields on the right (**25min**). A minute later, on joining a concrete lane, turn left (signpost: EL FAYAL, PUNTAGORDA, GR130, CAMINO REAL DE LA COSTA). Some 20m/yds downhill, turn right on a track (signpost: LAS BURACAS, ST DOMINGO). When this track ends, the old path becomes your way again, lined at the left by small country dwellings. Crossing a small *barranco,* you gain a first view of some large dragon trees on the hillside above.

This scattered little quarter of **Las Tricias** retains much of its original character. As you pass between some old homes with traditional high windows, chickens and cats scatter in all directions.

Emerging from the houses, you descend to the Las Tricias road (SIGNPOST), below the village centre. Cross a smaller road going left here and make your way down the main road to the right. A little over five minutes down the road (**45min**), just before it curves to the right, take the first cobbled lane on the left (signpost: LAS BURACAS, ST DOMINGO). It passes between two houses, and you

Dragon trees at Las Tricias, not far beyond the windmill shown on page 2

come onto a track. Two minutes down the track, you pass through an intersection, and asphalt comes under foot. Just past the first house on the right, take the cobbled path descending to the right (signpost: 'RT TRAVIESA'). A minute down, opposite a house named LA CASA BLANCA, rejoin the road and follow it downhill for just over 100m/yds. At this point, where the road bends right, turn left on a track running along the edge of Barranco de Izcagua, ignoring the signposted path at the very beginning of this track. The track quickly peters out into a narrow path. Keeping straight down, pass rustic cottages set amidst colourful gardens and fruit trees. Although the hillsides are cultivated, they have a dishevelled appearance. More dragon trees appear.

Reach the road and turn left, making for an old wind-mill standing on the hilltop ahead (photograph page 2), by following the road to the left, then ascending a chained-off track on the right. A good vista awaits you from the WINDMILL (**1h05min**): the ridges flatten out on their descent before finally dropping into the sea. The ridge to the north is the refuge for the island's biggest concentration of dragon trees. Humble cottages lean up against the rocky ridge.

From here on a maze of paths will lead you through cosy corners of countryside. Facing inland, with your back to the windmill, take the path on the top of the ridge, behind a yellow house, heading into prickly pear cacti. A minute down, on meeting a path, turn left along the left-hand side of a chicken run. Pass below an two houses, and ignore all minor side-paths. Before continuing, admire the enormous dragon trees to the left. Then carry straight on through someone's garden and the outdoor 'living rooms' of some inhabited caves. Scramble up a few metres to the main, beautifully cobbled path and follow it to the left; it descends the crest of the ridge and takes you past more dragon trees.

Your next stop is the Buracas Caves, soon to be seen in the far wall of the *barranco* to the right. A good ten minutes down the ridge on this manicured path (ignoring turn-offs), you pass some low cottage rooftops on your left. At a T-junction 50m/yds further on (signpost: CAFÉ FINCA ALOE), turn right and round the wall of the *barranco*. At the next junction, near this café-bar (which offers lovely light refreshments and health food), go right again. In a few minutes you're standing in front of the **Cuevas de Buracas** (**1h30min**). The main cave is really just an

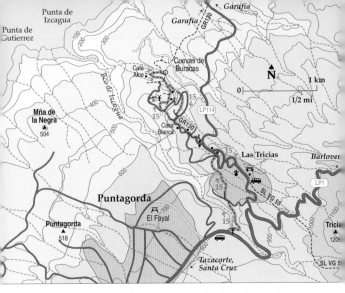

overhang of rock. It's not much to look at, but a short way up the path beyond it there are a few more (equally unspectacular) caves, and some rocks marked with petroglyphs.

Home is all uphill! Return to the ridge and ascend it, keeping to the crest. After 25 minutes you reach a track (SIGNPOST). Cross it (and the adjacent *canal*) and continue uphill on a cobbled path. You cross a road a minute later (SIGNPOST). Heading up through almond trees, pass under a massive dragon tree. Joining another track, turn 3m/yds left to the road and follow this back up to LA CASA BLANCA, now on your right. Ascend the cobbled path opposite, and return along your outward route. Once back on the LAS TRICIAS ROAD (**2h15min**), follow it uphill for five minutes, until you see a concrete lane ascending between two houses on your left. Climb the lane and rejoin the road. Some 100m/yds up the road, turn left on another concrete lane ascending the hillside, probably with a couple of crabby little dogs at your heels. You rejoin the road just 150m/yds below the village shop/ bar in **Las Tricias** (**2h35min**); follow the road up to the left, to the BUS STOP in front of the village shop.

Walk 16: GARAFIA • EL PALMAR • JUAN ADALID • EL PALMAR • GARAFIA

Distance: 13km/8mi; 4h05min

Grade: moderate, with ascents/descents of 400m/1300ft overall. Some short stretches demand a head for heights. Not recommended in wet weather. Can be extremely windy. *Red and white GR and yellow/white PR waymarking in the first 30 minutes*

Equipment: walking boots, sunhat, sunglasses, suncream, warm jacket, raingear, picnic, plenty of water

How to get there and return: 🚌 from Los Llanos to/from Garafía (Línea 2); journey time 1h45min. The return bus leaves Garafía from alongside the Casa de Cultura, a large building at the village entrance. Or 🚗: park in Garafía near the *plaza*. Local taxi tel: (+34) 630-450560

Short walk: Garafía — El Palmar — Garafía (6.25km/3.9mi; 1h40min). Easy, with ascents/descents of 200m/650ft overall. Otherwise grade, equipment and access as main walk. Follow the main walk to El Palmar and return the same way.

The north of the island remains relatively untouched by tourism. Being far from the main tourist centres, it hasn't become a hiking highway like the Ruta de los Volcanes or the Caldera de Taburiente. It's wild and rugged, with villages few and far between.

You leave the bus in **Garafía** at the turning for the village centre. From the BUS STOP walk straight to the *plaza* (main square). The church is worth a visit if you have the time (see touring notes on page 18). Then locate the **Mirador el Chorro** behind the church, where **the walk begins**. (It's opposite a strange three-storey building, the old pharmacy, and there's a large, confusing sign here in three languages; read the part for the GR130.) Follow the small road uphill past the *mirador* for 50m/yds, then turn left on a cobbled path descending into the **Barranco de la Luz** (signpost: EL PALMAR, BARLOVENTO, GR130, CAMINO REAL DE LA COSTA). First you'll notice the dragon trees. Large clumps of the cacti-like candelabra spurge grow out of the *barranco* walls too.

The path crosses the bed of the *barranco* and climbs out the far side (this ascent may be unnerving for those who have no head for heights). You pass a number of caves with goats and two houses built into the hillside, and emerge on the end of a CONCRETE TRACK (**10min**). Keep ahead on the track for two minutes, then turn right on a path. Two minutes later, back on the track (no longer concreted, but with a SIGNPOST), turn right but, after under 20m/yds, pick up the old *camino* again, below the track (SIGNPOST). You pass through two wooden gates; please close them behind you. You round the hillside,

At about 35 minutes into the walk, approaching El Palmar, you look across the northwest corner of the island (left) and may spot a lonely billy goat (right). A corral lies just below the path at this point (far right).

passing through traces of terracing. Open and spacious, devoid of settlement and with windswept vegetation, this is La Palma's 'wild (north)west'. Soon the rocky shoreline comes into view.

Passing above an uninhabited homestead, descend to a track and follow it to the right for 10m/yds. Then pick up the path again, straight ahead — in places it's a beautifully built old stone-laid trail. Solitary houses dot the sides of ridges. The terrain is rocky; little grows here except for the usual xerophytic vegetation. Ascend to a narrow road (**35min**; SIGNPOST). Follow this downhill to the left. Two minutes down, turn right to rejoin the old path. Two minutes further along, when you are overlooking a homestead, the way forks. Take the right fork. The *barranco* here is full of candelabra spurge.

On the bend just before the homestead, ascend the path to the right (signpost: DON PEDRO), walking alongside a small *casita*. A few renovated and derelict cottages lie below. This is **El Palmar**, and soon you arrive at the edge of the deep **Barranco El Palmar** (**50min**). *(The Short walk returns from here.)*

Now descend into the ravine. Approaching the floor of the *barranco,* keep left. Then walk along the stream bed to

the right, to a *fuente* (spring) hidden behind enormous yam leaves. The water is refreshingly cool but, unfortunately, the spring is dry in summer.

From the *fuente* return along the *barranco* bed for 10m/yds, where your path out of the *barranco* ascends to the right. Climbing the wall of this ravine, you pass several caves. A stiff climb takes you up to a COUPLE OF BUILDINGS (**1h10min**). Pass above them and, two minutes later, walk behind another house. Don't forget to enjoy the view behind you: a pleasant feeling of isolation spreads over these hills. A minute later you join a minor, unused track. The few houses you can see strung out along the edge of the *barranco* opposite comprise the hamlet of El Mudo, now virtually abandoned. A few minutes along, the path joins a minor track: keep left (SIGNPOST). The tops of wind generators now appear over the crests of the ridges ahead. Some five minutes later, you come to the MAIN TRACK (**1h25min**) that descends to El Mudo (signpost: JUAN ADALID, BARLOVENTO). Follow this track to the right uphill for a minute, then rejoin your path (SIGNPOST). The surrounding hillsides are covered in cistus and heather.

One final, deep ravine follows — the **Barranco Domingo Diaz**. A blade of ridge jutting into the sea below, surmounted by a chapel, catches your attention on this fairly vertiginous, but amply wide path. Amazingly enough there's a track up to the chapel. At the bottom of the *barranco*, as you are entering an enclosure, please leave the GATE as you find it (**1h55min**). Climbing out of the *barranco*, the way is blocked by fences and another gate. Go through the gate (again leaving it as you find it) and

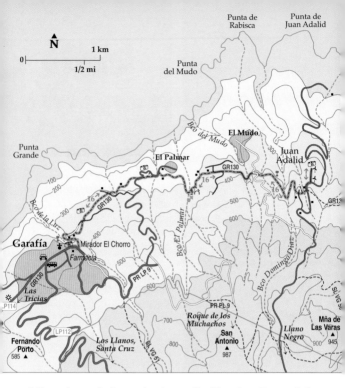

follow the path through a 'tunnel' of heather. Beyond the heather and past a house, you look across a shallow gully onto a couple of farm houses dwarfed by two giant wind generators. Quite a sight! Cross a farm track, and dip into the gully, ignoring the turning to the left.

Passing to the right of a house, the path arrives at a road in an area called **Juan Adalid** (signpost: DON PEDRO, BARLOVENTO). Turn left downhill, then turn left again on the track to the WIND GENERATORS and climb the HILLOCK beyond them (**2h 10min**). If there isn't a gale blowing, this is the perfect spot for a picnic. A couple of lonely outposts lie on a coastal shelf below. Looking across the northern coastline, severed by sheer cliffs, the village to the east is Gallegos (Walk 1).

From here retrace your outward route back to **Garafía** (**4h05min**).

Walk 17: PISTA AL DERRABADO • (FUENTE DE MENCAFETE) • SABINOSA • ERMITA DE LA VIRGEN DE LOS REYES • SABINOSA

Distance/time: 15km/9.5mi; 5h40min

Grade: very strenuous, with an ascent of about 700m/2300ft and descents of 1300m/4250ft overall. You must be sure-footed and have a head for heights. Don't attempt in wet weather. It can be very windy and cold on this walk, and the *cumbre* is often covered in cloud. *White/yellow PR waymarking most of the way*

Equipment: walking boots, sunhat, sunglasses, suncream, long-sleeved shirt, long trousers, jacket, anorak, raingear, picnic, plenty of water

How to get there: 🚕 taxi or with friends to the Pista al Derrabado
To return: 🚌 from Sabinosa (Ruta 4); departs at about 14.10 and 16.10 *Mon-Sat only;* or telephone to Tigaday for a taxi from the bar in Sabinosa

Short walks

1 **Pista al Derrabado — Sabinosa** (6.5km/4mi; 2h05min). Quite easy, with a descent of 600m/2000ft. Short stretches demand a head for heights, otherwise grade as main walk. Access, equipment and return as main walk, but stout shoes will suffice. Follow the main walk to Sabinosa, the 2h05min-point.

2 **Sabinosa — Ermita de la Virgen de los Reyes — Sabinosa** (8.5km/5mi; 3h35min). Very strenuous, with an ascent of 650m/2100ft. Grade and equipment as main walk. Access by 🚕 to Sabinosa. Join the walk at the 2h05min-point and follow it to the end.

This far-flung corner of the island is for me the most beautiful part of El Hierro. Once over the cloud-enshrouded *cumbre*, and no longer battered by wind, you can traipse across a little corner of the island's 'Cornwall', where sheep and cows are the only company you'll have. If you're not made of marathon material, the two short walks are both well worth considering.

Start the walk at the junction with a track, the **Pista al Derrabado** (signposted 'FUENTE DE MENCAFETE'). From here you have a splendid view across the banana and

Ermita de la Virgen de los Reyes

pineapple plantations of El Golfo to the rocky islets of Salmor. **Set off** by following this track: it gradually descends around the sheer face of the escarpment, into the **El Golfo** crater. The hills are thickly wooded in laurel. The western part of the crater is bare of life save for the veins of stone walls that cross it. A spa, the Pozo de la Salud, is marked by a large, prominent building standing above the sea (photograph page 31). At one point (**35min**) you have an uninterrupted view through a gap in the vegetation over the western wing of the crater. Pass through farmland set on shelves high in the wall of the *cumbre*. A good 20 minutes later, a path joins you from the left. Some 200m/yds further on, at a fork, go left (signposted 'FUENTE MENCAFETE' and 'CAMINO SABINOSA').

Attention: Around five minutes uphill, an ENCLOSED PROPERTY sits off the track to the right (**1h**). Just beyond it, be sure to leave the track, following a grassy overgrown path downhill (signpost: 'SABINOSA, PR EH1'). Five minutes later, a path goes left to the Fuente de Mencafete, a possible short detour. Round a steep hillside; you will remain on this path all the way to Sabinosa: ignore a number of minor paths turning off. You come to a stone bench with a sign indicating that this is the 'KING'S STONE'

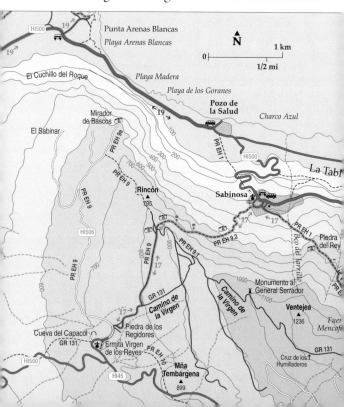

(**Piedra del Rey**; 1h20min) — a good rest stop. Just past it, as you round a bend, a bird's-eye view unfolds down onto the picturesque but rather severe looking Sabinosa, atop a volcanic mound that protrudes from the crater wall. The dark volcanic slopes that surround it are patched in vineyards. The descent of these gravel slopes may prove slightly unnerving for some.

When you reach a street in **Sabinosa** (2h) keep straight ahead to CAMINO LA DEHESA. Then go right downhill on CALLE HOYA DEL MORAL (the lower half of Camino la Dehesa). At the *plaza* turn right to the friendly local, BAR SABINOSA (2h05min), to revive yourself for the tough ascent ahead. *(Short walk 1 ends here, and Short walk 2 begins here.)*

Return to CAMINO LA DEHESA and now climb it. It circles above the village. Just where it begins to descend, turn left uphill on a well-maintained path signposted 'CAMINO A LA DEHESA' (yellow/white waymarking). A steep climb through vineyards and then heather follows, with no turn-offs to worry about. Dark green junipers dot the lower inclines. Don't forget to enjoy the views behind you. On reaching the tree-heather and evergreen zone, you may be enveloped in cloud — notice the rocks and tree

trunks beside the path, thick with moss. Nearing the *cumbre* the way is again slightly vertiginous. This is where you feel the full brunt of the wind, too.

Just over the CREST (**3h 20min**), by a spring on the left, you meet the end of a track. You overlook a pastoral landscape here, littered with old lichen-clad stone walls. Below to the right, clumps of pines make a half-hearted attempt to forest an uneven basin. If you have any energy left, make for these pines — out of the wind and, with luck, in the sun — as idyllic a spot as you'll find on the island.

To continue to the Ermita de la Virgen de los Reyes, cross a track and then keep straight down, ignoring a track to the right. Some 15 minutes along, take a rough track descending to the right (the **Camino de la Virgen**; signposted).

You reach the **Piedra de los Regidores** at a junction of tracks. (Every four years, the July 'Bajada de la Virgin' begins here at dawn.) A right turn here leads to the Mirador de Basco and El Sabinar. Take the second track to the left (white/red waymarking). The track cuts through an old crater. Five minutes along, just after the road becomes surfaced, turn left down a paved walkway to the **Ermita de la Virgen de los Reyes** (**3h55min**), home of the island's patron saint.

From here retrace your steps back to **Sabinosa**, allowing about 1h45min for the return (**5h40min**).

Top: in the heather and evergreen zone, on the ascent to the Ermita de la Virgen de los Reyes. Bottom: view down over Sabinosa on the descent from the Pista al Derrabado

Walk 18: FRONTERA • MIRADOR DE JINAMA • ERMITA VIRGEN DE LA PEÑA • MIRADOR DE LA PEÑA

See also photograph page 10

Distance/time: 10km/6.2mi; 3h50min

Grade: strenuous, with an ascent of 900m/3000ft and a descent of 500m/1640ft. You must be sure-footed and have a head for heights. The walk is only worth the effort on clear fine days. Take care when crossing any loose gravel, whether it is on the path itself or the result of a landslide. Don't attempt after heavy rain; there is a danger of rockfall. It can be very windy and cold on the top of the *cumbre*.

Equipment: walking boots, sunhat (tied on!), sunglasses, suncream, long-sleeved shirt, long trousers, walking stick(s), warm cardigan, anorak, raingear, picnic, plenty of water

How to get there: 🚕 by taxi or with friends to Frontera (or walk there from the Tigaday/Las Puntas junction)
To return: 🚌 (Ruta 5) from the Mirador de la Peña (convenient departures at about 16.30, 18.15 Mon-Fri) or 🚕 telephone for a taxi

Short walk: Mirador de Jinama — Frontera (3.2km/2mi; 1h25min). Easy, but steep descent of 900m/3000ft. Otherwise grade and equipment as main walk. Access 🚕 by taxi or with friends to the Mirador de Jinama. Descend the signposted path to Frontera. Use the map to do the main walk in reverse. Return by 🚌 from Frontera, or call a taxi from Tigaday

Alternative walk: Frontera — Mirador de Jinama — San Andrés (8km/5mi; 2h50min). Ascent, equipment, access as main walk. Return by 🚌 from San Andrés (Rutas 2 and 8) or telephone a Tigaday taxi from there. Follow the main walk to the country road beyond the Mirador de Jinama. Seven minutes along this road, turn right on a wide path signposted 'PR EH8, San Andrés' (white-yellow waymarking). Some 30min from the road, and shortly after the path has widened to a track, turn right at a fork. Two minutes later, when a track joins you from the right, follow it to the left (signposted 'GR131, Tiñor–Valverde, Camino de la Virgen'). Just around the bend, turn right on another track. Several minutes later, cross the Guarazoca road and enter San Andrés, passing the school and the church. The bus stop is outside the shop on the left, where you meet the main HI1 (convenient departures 14.35 16.35 *Mon-Fri only*).

This hike is one long view. From beginning to end you overlook the most stunning bay of the archipelago, El Golfo. And if that's not enough, the magnificent path underfoot is one of the most breathtaking in all the Canaries ... both literally and visually.

Start the walk in the tiny village of **Frontera**: take the small road between the two bars opposite the church. At the fork 10m/yds uphill, keep left, following the sign 'JINAMA 3.4KM'. A steep narrow road takes you up a hillside stepped with vineyards. An amphitheatre of precipitous walls encircling the entire bay rises up before you. Your path will climb this very wall! A couple of minutes after passing a parking area with a couple of benches,

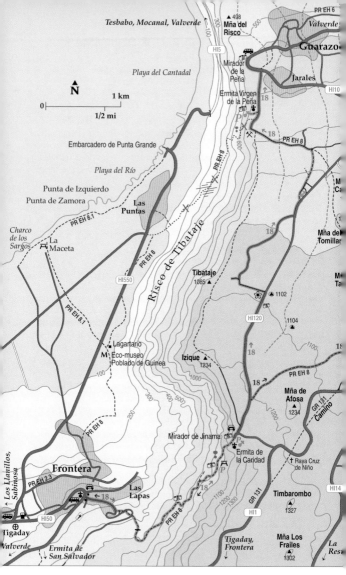

the road bends sharp right (**10min**). At the bend, turn left up a wide cobbled path (signposted). This fine centuries-old trail will take you up to the *mirador*. At a fork keep left and, on reaching the road again, go left for 20m/yds, then rejoin your path. Thick stone walls flank the *camino*. Cross the road one last time, by a sign, 'CAMINO DE JINAMAR' (**20min**).

Above the vineyards the route dives into shady laurel woods. The higher the climb, the more striking the views. The distant splash of white, high up the mountain wall

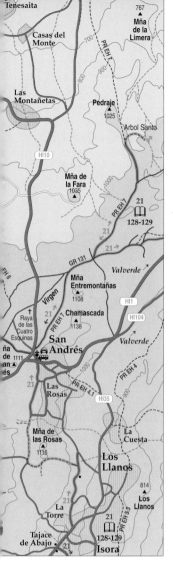

near the end of the *cumbre,* is Sabinosa. The path, a work of art, ascends in a string of tortuous Zs. Here the precipitous cliffs are home to some rare endemics: *Bencomia sphaerocarpa, Crambe strigosa* and *Sideritis canariensis,* as well as the more common *Echium strictum* and *Aeonium holochrysum.*

A BALCONY VIEWPOINT (**1h20min**) makes a good rest stop, looking across the coastal plain of *malpais.* Pineapples are cultivated in the numerous greenhouses spread across it. The surrounding vegetation drips with moss and lichen. After ignoring a minor fork to the left, as you near the summit, a couple of unstable-looking stone tables and benches at a hillside *mirador* (**1h50min**) provide a superb view over the gulf, framed by the *cumbre.* Fifteen minutes later, you reach the **Mirador de Jinama** (**2h05min**; Picnic 18a), with a fountain (sometimes dry) in the hillside on the right, to the right of a chapel, the **Ermita de la Caridad**. *(The Short walk begins here.)* From the *mirador* you enjoy a superb view out over the whole bay, a dark lava coastline with jagged indentations contrasting with the bright greens and blues of the sea. The *cumbre* sweeps back out of the bay into a high wall fringed in laurels and heather.

From here the way is all downhill. Follow the road away from the *mirador.* When it swings right towards the main road, continue straight on along a country road. *(The Alternative walk turns right off this road after seven minutes.)*

Now you're on the roof of the island, looking across a sloping plateau ruptured by a multitude of small volcanic cones. A maze of stone walls criss-cross the landscape. Thirty minutes down the road, just after passing a fenced-off garden opposite a pint-sized VOLCANO (a good viewpoint; **2h35min**), turn left along a wide track. The track bumps its way between walled-off fields and grazing land, with the occasional plot of corn or potatoes.

Some five minutes along, the track bends right and acquires a tarmac surface, On meeting the ROAD again (**3h05min**), follow it to the left downhill for 200m/yds,

The centuries-old trail to the Mirador de Jinama

View down onto the Roques de Salmor from the rim of the crater (near Picnic 18b)

then pick up your continuing path, which passes behind a MASSIVE WATER TANK. A minute along you meet a track coming from the right and follow it straight on, ignoring a track to the right after 50m/yds. When the track ends, go straight ahead, to pick up the old *camino* (between high stone walls). At the fork ahead, keep right on the main path. A few houses of Guarazoca can now be seen on the hillsides far below.

Less than 20 minutes from the road, you drop down onto a colourful, pink and mauve earthen track (signpost 'LA PEÑA, PR EH8'). Follow it to the left, and a good 10 minutes later (having ignored all side-paths, tracks and roads), you pass below an old quarry (**3h35min**). Turn right here, down an asphalt lane at the edge of the crater.* Continue down the lane for another minute to the **Ermita Virgen de la Peña**, tucked into the side of the cliff just below. This chapel is a superb quiet spot from which to enjoy the immense panorama (Picnic 18b; photograph page 10).

From here continue down to the Mirador de la Peña, which you can see from here — a cliff-hanging building housing a bar and restaurant, one of the most beautiful and impressive viewpoints in the Canarian archipelago. Follow the concrete lane down to the road, 15 minutes away, and turn left. Treat yourself to a well-earned drink at the **Mirador de la Peña** (**3h50min**), before telephoning for a tax or catching the bus (Línea 5) at the entrance to the *mirador*.

*Some 45m/yds along you pass a path off left; it used to be part of the PR EH8, and is still shown on many maps as a viable path. *Do not* attempt to descend this path, *it is broken away by landslides and exceedingly dangerous.*

Walk 19: COASTAL WALK AT ARENAS BLANCAS

Distance: 3.8km/2.4mi; 1h10min *by car*; 9km/5.6mi; 2h20min *by bus*

Grade: easy, flat; *recommended for everyone*. The path is far enough away from the waves to be safe, but spray may reach the path on a rough day. *But do not leave the path;* the coastline itself is crumbly and unstable.

Equipment: walking shoes, cardigan, water

How to get there and return: 🚗 to/from the signposted 'Arenas Blancas' parking area on the HI500 (the 14.6km-point in the car tour). Or 🚌 (Ruta 4; convenient departures/returns; see timetable page 133) to/from Pozo de la Salud and walk along the very quiet road to the Arenas Blancas parking area (allow an extra 2.6km/35min *each way*)

This spectacular coastal path is really for everyone! Impressive lava formations, coastal arches, blow holes and weird rocks accompany you on the first leg of the walk; steep cliffs and a view of El Golfo fill the backdrop on the second part.

Start off at the signposted PARKING AREA FOR ARENAS BLANCAS by following the clear track towards the coast. On the right is the small beach of **Arenas Blancas** with golden yellow sand. In the distance is the arc of El Golfo and nearby, on the black and bleak coastline the spa hotel of Pozo de la Salud. At a first fork, keep right; then, 50m/yds further on, keep left. The track now loops back to the left, and a clear stone-lined coastal path runs forward along the rocky cliffs. (This path will eventually form part of a GR coastal route round the island, but at time of writing is neither signposted nor waymarked.)

Follow this path to the left. After a few minutes you pass a large BLOW HOLE on the right (**10min**). Then the path moves inland for a while, to round a beautiful inlet. Another inlet follows (**20min**). Then you come to an

At the start of the walk

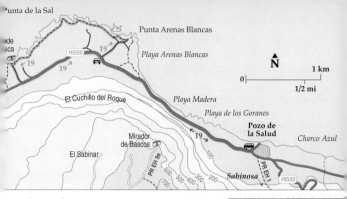

elevated LAVA STREAM (**25min**), where path rises and falls a little, crossing this tremendous lava flow.

Ten minutes later you pass through a *kipuka* (**35min**) — a patch spared by the lava, where an abundance of the original vegetation flourishes: saltwort (*Schizogyne sericea*), sea fennel (*Astydamia latifolia*), and sea lavender (*Limonium pectinatum*).

Ten minutes later you pass some stone-lined fields on your left. A lovely *mirador* on a cliff, overlooking a large sea-arch, the **Arco de la Tosca**, is on your right (**45min**). Here a track meets you from the left. Follow it down to the Playa del Verodal road, and turn left.

Walk back along this quiet road to the BLANCAS PARKING AREA (**1h10min**) — or continue on to **Pozo de la Salud** for your bus (add another 35min).

From top to bottom:
the kipuka, *full of greenery;*
one of the inlets;
Arco de la Tosca

121

Walk 20: HI1 • MIRADOR DEL LA LLANIA • HOYA DE FILEBA • FUENTE DEL LOMO • BAILADERO DE LAS BRUJAS • HI1

Distance: 5km/3mi; 1h10min

Grade: easy, with an ascent of less than 100m/330ft; suitable for all fit people

Equipment: walking shoes, warm cardigan, jacket, long trousers, raingear, water

How to get there and return: 🚗 by car only: park alongside the HI1 at the turn-off to the Ermita Virgen de los Reyes.

This short hike is El Hierro's little gem. It starts with yet another stupendous view over the gulf — a view of which I never tire. Then it wanders in and out of 'fairy-tale' woods, where you feel you've stepped centuries back in time. Moss envelops the trees and thickly carpets the ground. And the crater of Hoya de Fileba comes as a pleasant surprise.

Start out on the HI1 at the JUNCTION FOR THE ERMITA DE LA VIRGEN DE LOS REYES. Cross the road and follow the path signposted 'MIRADOR DE LA LLANIA' into the tall tree-heather. A short climb leads up to the **Mirador de la Llanía** (**5min**; Picnic 20), a superb vantage point looking down over the line of villages strung out along the foot of the *cumbre*. The forested walls of the crater stretch out impressively on either side. Just before you reach the viewpoint, notice a large stone column with a signpost on it.

From this bald piece of gravelly hillside, go back to the signpost and turn left for 'BAILADERO DE LAS BRUJAS' (the Witches' Dancing Ground). The path edges its way through a small wood, the vegetation dripping with lichen and moss. Out on the *lapilli*-covered slopes again, ignore a path ascending to the left. Barely a minute further down this steep slope, the path swings left to dip down into a small hollow of pine trees. Here, at a signposted junction, keep straight ahead, taking a zig and a zag up a steep slope, to the edge of a deepish crater — the **Hoya de Fileba**

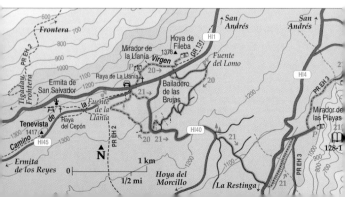

View over El Golfo from the Mirador de la Llanía (Picnic 19)

(**15min**). This charcoal-grey crater is speckled with heather.

Return to the signpost and now turn left for 'FUENTE DEL LOMO'. Look a short way along the road to the right, for a culvert. Walk through the culvert, then ascend the embankment on the left and continue along the path. Join a track and follow it to the right, to be greeted in a few minutes by a water tank — the **Fuente del Lomo**. Unlike any other spring I've come across, you step *down* into this one.

With your back to the tank, take the path to the right, following a sign for 'PISTA EL BREZAL' (orange arrow). The slopes above the path are cushion-soft with moss, tempting you run your hands over the inclines. At a crossing, with signpost and arrows, go left. Mounting a slight rise, an old track with stones placed intermittently on either side comes underfoot. When you come to a cool grassy clearing with a signpost, cross a wide path and continue straight ahead on the right-hand side of the clearing along a track lined with stones. Follow this track, ignoring all side-paths and tracks, until it dips down into a gully. Just opposite a signpost with arrows, take a narrow path off to the right.

You cross a WOODEN BRIDGE (**45min**). The vegetation changes and patches of laurel forest take over from the heather. Not far beyond the bridge, you cross the HOYA DEL MORCILLO ROAD and continue on the path signposted 'LA LLANÍA'. At the fork that follows, wind your way up to the right. Ignore a path to the left as you follow a small gully running alongside on the right. Another junction follows: keep right and follow the path back to the junction on the HI1 (**1h10min**), just where the walk began.

Back at your starting point on the road to the Ermita de la Virgen de los Reyes, you may like to follow the road to the left for 0.7km, to enjoy a spectacular view of the volcanic landscape (add 20min).

Walk 21: HI1 • MIRADOR DE LAS PLAYAS • LA TORRE • SAN ANDRÉS • ARBOL SANTO • TIÑOR

Distance/time: 18km/11mi; 4h55min

Grade: easy but very long, with short ascents of about 200m/650ft overall. Suitable for anyone who is fairly fit. *Note:* these highlands can often disappear under cloud and mists, and it can be cold and windy; the walk is best kept for fine, cloudless days.

Equipment: walking boots, sunhat, suncream, raingear, long-sleeved shirt, long trousers, warm cardigan, anorak, swimwear, picnic, plenty of water

How to get there: 🚖 by taxi or with friends to the turn-off for the Ermita de la Virgen de los Reyes on the HI1
To return: 🚌 (Ruta 2) from Tiñor (convenient departure 16.40 *Mon-Fri only*) or 🚖 prearrange for a taxi to collect you from the junction of the HI1 and the road into Tiñor, on the north side of the village.

Short walk: San Andrés — Arbol Santo — San Andrés (8km/5mi; 1h50min). Easy; equipment as above, but walking shoes will suffice. The above weather conditions apply. 🚌 Rutas 2 and 8 to/from San Andrés. By 🚖: park in San Andrés. Follow the main walk from San Andrés (the 3h-point) to the Arbol Santo, then return the same way.

Shorter walk: HI1 — Mirador de las Playas — La Torre — San Andrés (11km/6.75mi; 3h). Easy; equipment and access as main walk; return as the *Short walk*. Follow the main walk to San Andrés.

Alternative walk: HI1 — Mirador de Isora — *parador* (13km/8mi; 4h25min). Strenuous, with a steep, rough descent of 800m/2600ft from the *mirador* (tough on the knees). You must be sure-footed and have a head for heights. Do not attempt in wet or very windy weather. Yellow/white waymarking. Equipment and access as main walk; to return 🚌 Ruta 7 from the *parador* (departs *Mon-Fri only* at about 18.35) or telephone for a taxi. Follow the main walk to Tajace de Abajo (1h55min). As you come upon the houses, turn right immediately after building No 3 (opposite house No 4). There is a signpost here, 'PR EH3, Las Playas, La Cuesta, Vereda del Risco'. Follow an asphalted road straight downhill until you reach the road to the *mirador,* below Isora. Follow this road to the right for 10min, to the Mirador de Isora (2h25min). Your ongoing path (flanked by stone walls) begins on the far side of the viewpoint (signposted), and ascends to the crest opposite — then you begin the descent. A couple of minutes from the *mirador,* ignore a faint turning to the right. *Take utmost care* as you descend this very steep and slippery path, and leave any gates as you find them. Some 1h35min from the *mirador,* on entering the bed of the Barranco del Abra, the PR EH3 path goes off to the right. *Either* keep left downhill here on a faint path waymarked with white dots and small cairns. floundering in and out of the stream bed, or continue on PR EH3. When you meet the road by either route, the *parador* is a short way to the right.

This orange track, edged with asphodels, leads through bucolic countryside to the Arbol Santo.

The pine trees in El Pinar are among the most majestic in the archipelago. Just as bonsai is striking in its contrived, pint-sized beauty, so the *Pinus canariensis* is striking in its natural grandeur. From the heights of El Pinar you descend to another of El Hierro's picture-postcard *miradors*, before gradually climbing to a countryside where time stands still. If you're the adventurous type, I highly recommend the Alternative walk.

Start the walk at the TURN-OFF TO THE ERMITA (Santuario) DE LA VIRGEN DE LOS REYES. Just at the start of this road, take the path to the left signposted 'SENDERO DE LA LLANIA'. Follow the green arrows of this circular walk to where it crosses the HOYA DEL MORCILLO ROAD. (If you would like to spend an extra 20 minutes in this fairy-tale forest, follow the RED AND BLUE ARROWS, to make an extra loop back to the Hoya del Morcillo road — the western part of Walk 20.)

Join the road and turn right for 15 minutes. By several LARGE PINES (**30min**), note a track turning left into the forest. Pass it by but, 90m/yds below it, at a bend in the road, turn left on a minor track. After 50m/yds, at a fork, go left. You dip into a hollow to the left, then mount a second, parallel crest. A track joins from the left; keep downhill. This track will take you straight down to the El Pinar road. (Even if you lose trace of the track, just keep straight down to reach the road.) In this cool, shady forest, grand pines surround you. The forest floor is 'whistle-clean', a characteristic of a true Canary wood. A little over five minutes down the track, cross a *canal*. Less than 10 minutes later you cross the EL PINAR ROAD (HI4): keep straight on towards the stone wall ahead, crossing a water pipe en route. Then turn left alongside the wall and, without a path, remain between the pipe and the wall (closer to the pipe in the last few metres) until, after 15 minutes, you meet the ROAD TO THE MIRADOR DE LAS PLAYAS. Turn right here, passing the turn-off right for the PR EH3 to Las Casas after 100m/yds. A few minutes later you reach the **Mirador de las Playas** (**1h10min**; Picnic 21). The narrow curving bay set at the foot of 1000m/3300ft-high eroded cliffs is Las Playas. The *parador* is an obvious landmark in this desolate, isolated corner of the island, also shown below and on the cover.

From the *mirador* return along the road for 200m/yds, then turn right on a path signposted 'PR EH3 LAS PLAYAS, LA CUESTA'; this initially dips down, before heading uphill between stone walls. The small evergreen shrub predominant in the fields here is white broom (*escabon*). Less than 20 minutes from the *mirador* you join a track very near the edge of the cliff. This becomes asphalted and soon ascends to a ROAD (**1h40min**; signpost: 'PR EH3 LAS PLAYAS, LA CUESTA'). Turn right on the road and, a minute along, turn right again to climb

Alternative walk 21: plunging view from the Mirador de Isora down onto the isolated Playas, a curving line of stony beaches hidden in the sheer coastline. The parador *and a few solitary houses are the sole occupants of this barren, inhospitable stretch of arcing coastline.*

Crossing the plateau through walled-in pastures, on the approach to San Andrés

nearby **Montaña Bermeja**, an orange volcanic mound. From its summit there are fine views over the farming village of Isora on the slopes ahead.

You will now continue along this quiet country road for around 30 minutes, to La Torre. *(But if you are doing the Alternative walk, turn off the road about 20 minutes downhill, opposite house No 4 in Tajace de Abajo.).* In **La Torre** (**2h10min**) you cross a concrete ford in the road. Barely two minutes later, turn left along a road called CALLE LA LADERA. When you join a road ascending from the right, continue uphill. Some 15 minutes from La Torre (**2h25min**), 150m/yds past a beautiful, isolated *casa rural*, take the first left, a track ascending a narrow *barranco*. A minute up, an old cobbled *camino* becomes your way. The path climbs alongside the gully, before entering it briefly. Two minutes up the gully, leave it (beside a volcanic cone), and continue left as the path crosses a plateau. Ignore a turn-off left (**2h45min**). The path widens into a track. When you meet the road, turn right onto the wide path. Walled-in pastures stretch across this tableland. San Andrés comes into sight across the stone walls, spread around the base of a volcanic cone.

Soon you reach a wide dry stream bed: turn right here. Then, a little further on, come to a road and turn left. Follow this road until you reach another road on the edge of **San Andrés**. Go left here and, after a few minutes, you come to the MAIN ROAD (**3h05min**). I enjoy the noisy back-slapping BAR LA IGUALDAD along to the right. *(The Short walk starts here, and both the Short walk and the Shorter walk end here.)*

Leaving San Andrés (from Bar La Igualdad), cross the road and follow it to the west (left), then take the first street (CALLE LA IGLESIA) to the right. Follow it to the LAS MONTAÑETAS ROAD and turn right. After 150m/yds, turn right on a wide track (SIGNPOST), soon passing a row of volcanic cones on the right. You come to a junction: keep right (signpost: 'GR131, PR EH7, TIÑOR, VALVERDE, EL GAROE, EL MOCANAL, LA CALCOSA'). A little over five minutes later (**3h25min**), fork left uphill on asphalt (sign: ARBOL SANTO). *(Note that you will return to this junction after your visit.)* The way is tarred only for the first few minutes, then the beautiful earthen track shown on pages 124-125 becomes your way. A basin of stone walls lies below to the right, and on the left volcanic mounds grow out of a tilting plateau. After 20 minutes, at the next fork, go left downhill (signposted 'ARBOL SANTO/GAROE'). A tarred road leads you down to a parking area/visitor centre, from where a well-trodden path heads right, round the hillside to **El Garoé**, the site of the original 'holy tree' (**Arbol Santo; 3h55min**). Legend has it that the original tree, a *til* (indigenous laurel), was venerated by the native Bimbaches as their 'rain tree', because it condensed enough water from the mists to fill all their requirements. Remains of the cisterns that collected the water can still be seen on the hillside. *(The Short walk returns to San Andrés from here.)*

Now on the leg to Tiñor, return to the fork first encountered at the 3h25min-point (less than 30 minutes back; **4h25min**; signpost: 'GR131, TIÑOR, VALVERDE'). Turn sharp left here, across a sheltered basin. After a good

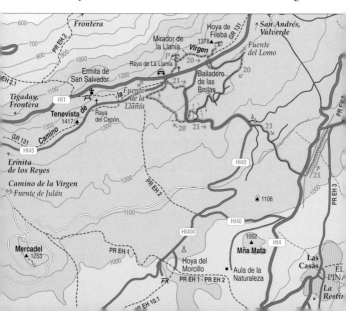

Top: near La Torre; bottom: El Pinar (left) and one of the old cisterns near the Arbol Santo.

five minutes, ignore a faint track to the left. Some 60m/yds further on, the Camino de la Virgen branches off to the left. Continue on for another 50m/yds and, at a staggered junction, first turn left off the main track and then, at the fork that follows, keep right along a cobbled trail. Above lie fields of *tagasaste* (broom); its branches are cut for animal fodder. Soon you cross the main road (HI1) and descend to **Tiñor**, a quiet hamlet tucked away in a concealed valley. Entering the village, pass the church and cross a road, to continue on the path, which descends to a driveway. Follow the drive back to the road, then keep straight on (right) for a couple of minutes, to regain the HI1 main road (**4h55min**). There is a bus stop just here, or pick up your taxi.

LA PALMA — BUSES

For a list of all 16 of the island's bus lines, with timetables and a good route map, see **www.transporteslapalma.com**. If you will be using the buses frequently, invest in a 'Bonobus' card (12 €); this will save about 20% on bus fares; several people can use the same card.

Line 1: Santa Cruz — El Paso — Los Llanos (via the *cumbre*)

Bus passes the visitors' centre about 35min from Santa Cruz, 15min from Los Llanos.

Departs Santa Cruz	Departs Los Llanos
06.00	05.00*
06.30*	05.30
and every 30 minutes on the hour and the half hour until	
22.00*	22.00*
22.45	22.30

Note that *buses on the half-hour from Santa Cruz only run Mon-Fri and buses on the hour from Los Llanos only run Mon-Fri*

Line 2: Santa Cruz — Los Llanos (via the north, usually with a change of bus in Barlovento)

Intermediate times are approximate! Bus calls at Tijarafe about 15min past Puntagorda en route to Tazacorte, calls about 30min past Tazacorte en route to Puntagorda

Santa Cruz	La Galga	Los Sauces	Barlovento	Gallegos	Puntagorda	Tazacorte	Los Llanos
			06.00*	06.15*	07.30	08.15	08.45
06.15	06.45	07.00	07.30*	07.45*	09.30*	10.15*	10.45*
07.15*	07.45*	08.00*a					
08.15	08.45	09.00	09.30*	09.45*	11.30	12.15	12.45
11.15*	12.00*a						
10.15	10.45	11.00	11.30	11.45	13.30*	14.15*	14.45*
12.15*	12.45*	13.00*	13.30*	13.45*	15.30*	16.15*	16.45*
13.15*	13.45*	14.00*a					
14.15	14.45	15.00	15.30*	15.45*	17.30*	18.15*	18.45*
15.15*	15.45*	16.00*a					
16.15	16.45	17.00	17.30*	17.45*	19.30	20.15	20.45
17.15*	17.45*	18.00*a					
18.15	18.45	19.00	19.30*	19.45b			
19.15*	19.45*	20.00*a					
20.15	20.45	23.00a					
21.15*	21.45*	22.00*a					

Los Llanos	Tazacorte	Puntagorda	Gallegos	Barlovento	Los Sauces	La Galga	Santa Cruz
				06.30*	06.50*	07.20*	07.50*
			06.45*	07.30	07.50	08.20	08.50
				08.30*	08.50*	09.20*	09.50*
06.15*	06.30*	07.30*	08.45*	09.30	09.50	10.20	10.50
				10.30*	10.50*	11.20*	11.50*
08.15	08.30	09.30	10.45	11.30	11.50	12.20	12.50
				12.30*	12.50*	13.20*	13.50*
10.15*	10.30*	11.30*	14.45*	13.30	13.50	14.20	14.50
				14.30*	14.50*	15.20*	15.50*
12.15	12.30	13.30	14.45*	15.30*	15.50*	16.20*	16.50*
				16.30*	16.50*	17.20*	17.50*
14.15*	14.30*	15.30*	16.45*	17.30	17.50	18.20	18.50
				18.30*	18.50*	19.20*	19.50*
16.15	16.30	17.30	18.45	19.30	19.50	20.20	20.50
				20.30*	20.50*	21.20*	21.50*

*Mon-Fri only; **not Sun or holidays; a terminates at Los Sauces; b terminates at Franceses, 15min from Gallegos

Line 3: Santa Cruz — Los Llanos (via Los Canarios, Fuencaliente, Mazo)

Buses depart Mazo approximately 20min from Santa Cruz, 55min from Los Llanos; Los Canarios 40min from Santa Cruz, 40min from Los Llanos; Fuencaliente 45min from Santa Cruz, 30min from Los LLanos

Departs Santa Cruz	Departs Los Llanos
06.00*	06.00*
08.00	08.00
10.15	10.00
12.00	12.00
13.15* (only to Mazo)	14.00
14.15	16.00*
16.00	18.00
18.00	20.00
20.15	
22.45	

13.15**	13.45**
13.45	14.15
14.15**	14.45**
14.45	15.15
15.15*	15.45*
15.45	16.15
16.15*	16.45*
16.45	17.15
17.15*	17.45*
17.45	18.15
18.15*	18.45*
18.45	19.15
19.15*	19.45*
19.45	20.15
20.15*	20.45*
20.45	21.15
21.15*	21.45*
21.45	22.15
22.15*	22.45*
22.45	23.15
23.45	00.15

Line 4: Los Llanos — Puerto Naos

Buses from Los Llanos go on to Charco Verde; buses from Puerto Naos depart from Charco Verde 10min earlier

Departs Los Llanos	Departs Puerto Naos
06.30**	07.00**
07.30**	08.00**
08.30	09.00
09.00**	09.30**
09.30	10.00
10.00**	10.30**
10.30	11.00
11.00**	11.30**
11.30	12.00
12.00**	12.30**
12.30	13.00
13.00**	13.30**
13.30	14.00
14.00**	14.30**
14.30	15.00
and every hour on the half hour daily until	*and every hour on the hour daily until*
22.30	23.00

Line 8: Santa Cruz — Airport

Departs Santa Cruz	Departs Airport
06.45	07.15
07.15**	07.45**
07.45	08.15
08.15**	08.45**
08.45	09.15
09.15**	09.45**
09.45	10.15
10.15**	10.45**
10.45	11.15
11.15**	11.45**
11.45	12.15
12.15**	12.45**
12.45	13.15

continues in the next column

Línea 12 Los Sauces — San Andrés

Departs Los Sauces	Departs San Andrés
07.10*	07.20*
09.10	09.20
11.10	11.20
12.10*	12.20*
14.00	14.10
17.10	17.20

Line 21: Los Llanos — Puerto de Tazacorte (via Tazacorte)

Departs Los Llanos	Departs Puerto Tazacorte
06.30**	07.00**
07.30**	08.00**
08.30	09.00
09.00*	09.30*
09.30	10.00
10.30	11.00
11.00*	11.30*
11.30	12.00
12.30	13.00
13.00*	13.30*
13.30	14.00
then every hour on the half hour daily until 22.30	*then every hour on the hour daily until 23.00*

Line 31: Los Canarios — Faro (via Las Indias)

Departs Los Canarios 09.45 and every two hours on the hour daily until 21.00 21.00	Departs Faro 09.00 and every two hours at 45min past the hour daily until 19.45

*Mon-Fri only; **not Sun or holidays

EL HIERRO — BUSES

Buses are run by the Sociedad Cooperativa de Transportes de Viajeros del Hierro (4, Calle El Molino, Valverde; www.transhierro.es). The website has an English version. As of press date, the website was a bit tedious to use, however, as there were no weekly timetables to view: one had to choose the specific date of travel to see bus times. However, there are good route maps showing all stops.

Ruta 1: Around Valverde

Mon-Sat only departs Valverde 07.45, 09.00, 10.00, 10.30, 12.00, 13.00, 13.30, 15.00*, 16.45*, 18.00*
* not on Saturdays

Ruta 2: Valverde to El Pinar via San Andrés and Tiñor

Monday-Friday

El Pinar	San Andrés	Valverde
07.10	07.20	07.35
11.00	11.10	11.35
14.30	14.40	15.05
16.45	16.55	17.20

Valverde	San Andrés	El Pinar
09.30	09.45	09.55
13.10	13.25	13.35
15.30	15.45	15.55
18.00	18.15	18.25

Saturdays

El Pinar	San Andrés	Valverde
07.10	07.20	07.35
11.00	11.10	11.35
13.00	13.20	13.35

Valverde	San Andrés	El Pinar
09.30	09.45	09.55
11.30	11.45	11.55
13.30	13.45	13.55

Sundays and holidays

El Pinar	San Andrés	Valverde
07.10	07.20	07.35
13.00	13.20	13.35

Valverde	San Andrés	El Pinar
09.30	09.45	09.55
13.30	13.45	13.55

Ruta 3: El Golfo to Valverde (from Frontera bus station, via Las Puntas)

Mon-Fri: Departs Frontera 07.15, 08.45, 11.15, 14.15, 16.15; journey time about 25min; departs Valverde 08.00, 10.30, 13.10, 15.00, 18.00

Sat, Sun and holidays: Departs Frontera 07.15, 08.45, 12.00; journey time about 25min; departs Valverde 08.00, 10.30, 13.30

Ruta 4: Around El Golfo, some buses to Sabinosa and Pozo de la Salud

Mon-Sat only

Departs **Sabinosa** for Frontera station at 07.00; departs Frontera station for **local trips** ('circunvalación') 07.30, then departs Frontera station for **Pozo de la Salud** at 08.30

Departs **Pozo de la Salud** for Frontera station 09.00; departs Frontera station for **local trips** ('circunvalación') at 09.30, then departs Frontera station for **Pozo de la Salud** at 11.00

Departs **Pozo de la Salud** for Frontera station at 11.30; departs Frontera station for **local trips** ('circunvalación') 12.00, 13.00, then departs Frontera station for **Sabinosa** at 13.40*

Departs **Sabinosa** for Frontera station at 14.00*, then departs Frontera station for **Pozo de la Salud** at 15.30*

Departs **Pozo de la Salud** for Frontera station at 16.00*; departs Frontera station for **local trips** ('circunvalación') at 16.30* and 17.30*

* As the code indicates, there are no Saturday buses after the local trips at 13.00

Ruta 5: Valverde — Isora (for Mirador de la Peña)
Departs Valverde *Mon-Fri* 08.00, 10.00, 13.10, 18.00; *Sat-Sun* 08.00, 10.00, 13.10
Departs Isora *Mon-Fri* 07.00, 09.00, 11.00, 16.00; *Sat-Sun* 07.00, 09.00, 11.00

Ruta 6: Valverde — La Calheta — Tamaduste — Airport
Daily departs Valverde 07.45, 10.30, 13.30, 16.45
Daily departs airport 08.45, 11.30, 15.00, 17.45

Ruta 7: Valverde — *Parador*
Departs Valverde *Mon-Fri* 08.00, 09.45, 13.10, 17.00; *Sat-Sun* 08.00, 09.45, 13.30
Departs *Parador Mon-Fri* 08.30, 10.25, 13.35, 17.30; *Sat-Sun* 08.30, 10.25, 13.55

Ruta 8: La Restinga — El Pinar
Dep La Restinga *Mon-Fri* 06.40, 10.30, 14.05, 16.30; *Sat* 06.40, 10.30, 12.30; *Sun* 06.40, 12.30
Dep El Pinar *Mon-Fri* 10.00, 13.40, 16.00, 18.30; *Sat* 10.00, 12.00, 14.00; *Sun* 10.00, 14.00

Ruta 9: Valverde — Enchedo — Pozo de las Calcosas
Dep Valverde *Mon-Fri* 07.00, 11.00, 16.00, 17.30; *Sat/Sun* 07.00, 11.00
Dep Pozo de las Calcosas *Mon-Fri* 07.20, 11.20, 16.20, 17.50; *Sat/Sun* 07.20, 11.20

FLIGHTS TO LA PALMA AND EL HIERRO

At time of writing there are **direct flights** from London Gatwick to **Santa Cruz de la Palma** on Fridays (Thompson) and Saturdays (Norwegian) *throughout the year*. Thompson also fly from Manchester. Flights via Madrid and Barcelona with Iberia and other carriers are another option. There are **no direct flights to El Hierro**, so those visiting *only* El Hierro usually fly via Tenerife or Gran Canaria. Almost all flights from the UK are into Reina Sofia airport in the *south* of Tenerife, whereas the Binter flights to El Hierro are out of Los Rodeos airport in the *north* (an expensive taxi transfer). See www.titsa.com for buses between the airports (lines 340/343) or local buses into Santa Cruz (line 111) and from there to Los Rodeos (lines 102, 107, 108). On Gran Canaria the same airport is used for entering international flights and ongoing local flights.

INTER-ISLAND TRAVEL

You can travel between the islands by air or ferry but, unfortunately, arrangements seem to change every year — some years the only direct connection is by air, other years by ferry.

By plane: At time of writing it is *not* possible to fly direct between the islands — one has to travel via Tenerife. Flights are frequent and connections good, making a total journey time of about two hours. Still, that compares very badly with the direct flights which used to run twice a week and take only 15-20 minutes!

Keep your eye on the website **www.bintercanarias.com**, to see if the direct flights have been resumed. All information about current flights via Tenerife is on the same website, and flights can be booked online — or contact your travel agent *before you go* (flights may be full if you wait until you are on the islands to book).

By ferry: At the time of writing the only ferry connection between La Palma and El Hierro is via Tenerife (Los Cristianos). Two ferry companies currently serve these routes: Naviera Armas (**www. naviera armas.com**) and Fred Olsen Lines (**www.fredolsen.es**). Ferry bookings can be made online, at travel agencies before you go or once you are on the islands — or at the ferry kiosks at the Santa Cruz and Valverde ports.

Index

This index contains geographical entries only; for other entries, see Contents, page 3. **Bold type** indicates a photograph; *italic type* indicates a map. Both may be in addition to a text reference on the same page. 'TT' refers to *timetable numbers* (see pages 131-134).

135